777493

WITHDRAWN

CITY OF
THE RIGHT

CITY OF THE RIGHT

Urban Applications of American Conservative Thought

Gerald L. Houseman

CONTRIBUTIONS IN POLITICAL SCIENCE, NUMBER 67

GREENWOOD PRESS
Westport, Connecticut • London, England

Library of Congress Cataloging in Publication Data

Houseman, Gerald L.
  City of the right.

  (Contributions in political science, ISSN 0147-1066;
no. 67)
  Bibliography: p.
  Includes index.
  1. Municipal government—United States. 2. Urban
policy—United States. 3. Conservatism—United States.
I. Title.   II. Series.
  JS323.H68   320.8'0973   81-6345
  ISBN 0-313-23181-8 (lib. bdg.)   AACR2

Library of Congress Catalog Card Number: 81-6345
ISBN: 0-313-23181-8
ISSN: 0147-1066

First published in 1982

Greenwood Press
A division of Congressional Information Service, Inc.
88 Post Road West
Westport, Connecticut 06881

Printed in the United States of America

10 9 8 7 6 5 4 3 2 1

Dedicated to
GEORGE CLARK LYON

CONTENTS

ACKNOWLEDGMENTS

Eugene Hogan of Western Washington University and James Jordan of the University of Ohio at Zanesville made several good suggestions about this project when it was first being developed. Thanks are also due to Robert Bock of Western New England College and Charles Redenius of Pennsylvania State University at Behrend. Tibor Machan of *Reason*, Santa Barbara, California, provided some interesting comments on Ayn Rand. The members of Richard Flathman's "Ethical Issues" seminar on "Authority and Citizenship," which met on two weekends in 1980 under sponsorship of the American Political Science Association, provided good insights. Becky Heagy was dedicated and helpful as a student research asistant. Christopher, Elisabeth, and Victoria Houseman are always helpful—well, almost always. And my wife, Penny, greatly encouraged me throughout this project.

CITY OF
THE RIGHT

THE LIBERALS' URBAN LEGACY

"SOVIET AID REQUESTED FOR BRONX" reads the *New York Times* headline in the Metropolitan Section of June 21, 1980. A city council member, guiding nine visiting Soviet officials through the rubble of the South Bronx, pointed out that President Jimmy Carter had visited the same spot, had pledged his help, and had now reneged. "What I am doing is asking the Soviet Government . . . for $5 billion in foreign aid to rebuild the South Bronx," the council member declared. This was a publicity ploy, of course, but it should not startle any observer of present-day urban America, for our cities are indeed in desperate straits.

The South Bronx, which has been visited since by President Ronald Reagan, has apparently become a perennial campaign stop as well as a symbol of urban failure and despair. Its only possible comfort is that it is not the only trouble spot. In 1980, riots erupted in Miami and Chattanooga, while many other cities recorded increased crime rates, higher levels of unemployment, a continuing decline in the quality of public services, and shameful conditions in the schools. Air and water quality are significant problems. Transit systems are operating hand-to-mouth, threatening to shut down despite steep fare increases. And businesses continue to move out of central cities, undermining the tax base and increasing joblessness and poverty.

The trends of the post-World War II years continue, and for the cities this can only be bad news. Probably no one has thought that the cities could ever return to the pinnacles of power and success they knew in the 1920s. But it now seems difficult to imagine what goals were sought by the array of Great Society programs enacted in the 1960s—rent subsidies, urban renewal, aid to schools, environmental measures, transportation programs and subsidies, poverty aid, legal assistance, VISTA, day-care centers, job retraining. The liberals in control of the federal government at that time, Congress as well as the executive branch, set up more than 100 grants-in-aid programs, and these grew to 600 by 1972.[1] Over the years, a variety of mandated programs have also been added, reducing the autonomy of local governments and creating fiscal headaches. Mayor Edward Koch of New York, who served in Congress during the 1960s and the 1970s, has achieved a measure of popularity by denouncing his own support of these programs at the time.[2] To meet these objections of centralization and money mandates, refinements have been added, such as the increased emphasis upon neighborhood-level decisions and the do-it-yourself approach of revenue-sharing. The perception remains, however, and it is almost universal, that little has been achieved.

For those who cherish or decry these welfare state programs because they redistribute income in favor of a greater equality, the results show that there is nothing to worry about. Income has not been redistributed because of these programs or for any other reason, except in a slight direction towards greater inequality. The top 5.0 percent of American families, in terms of income, increased their share of the national wealth from 14.4 percent to 15.7 percent between 1972 and 1980 while the lowest 20.0 percent saw its share decline from 5.5 percent to 5.2 percent. Any number of other studies and indices confirm these trends.[3]

Urban programs themselves have probably enriched the wealthy as much as they have helped the poor. Our health programs have been scandal-riddled at times. Urban renewal has helped many corporations make fortunes. Federal, state, and local tax breaks and incentives have accompanied urban programs in order to give businesses money to pursue noble urban policy purposes. And poverty program administrators are seldom known to live in poverty.

Liberal programs, in short, have failed, or at the very least, have not lived up to the expectations that brought them into being. Certainly there are some exceptions. Food stamps have helped to prevent nutritional deficiencies and even starvation. Head Start seems to receive good marks from most evaluators. The overall record, all the same, is wanting, a perception that has held sway for some time. The Liberal City remains a place of crime, pollution, wasted effort, and broken dreams.

The liberals' urban legacy has placed our cities in the hands of conservatives. Conservatives now take their turn at managing urban programs and, more importantly, at finding answers to our urban problems. Even before the Reagan election victory in 1980, the United States was tending to shift towards conservatism in public policy, in political attitudes, and in the development of a national philosophy of politics. National polls have demonstrated for some time that far more Americans prefer to describe themselves as "conservative" than as "liberal."[4] The nationwide tax revolt of recent years has explicitly conservative overtones and implications. The so-called New Right, which combines grass-roots appeal with religious fervor, is not all noise, though that impression is often created. Most importantly, the existing mood seems to say that the American public is weary of the upheavals wrought by the rebellions and changes of the 1960s and 1970s, the Watergate trauma, and the Vietnam War. A "return to normalcy," even if only a vain hope, is seen in the national preoccupation with nostalgia in popular culture. Double-digit inflation and skyrocketing energy prices have also taken their toll of the national psyche, giving a new impetus to fiscal austerity and cost-consciousness, attitudes generally associated with conservatism since New Deal days.

The new strength of conservatism will certainly affect America's cities, particularly the older urban centers of the Northeast and Midwest. The obvious question is, how will they be affected? They will be influenced, of course, by the currents of politics and policymaking and by *fortuna*, but they also appear certain to be affected by the ideas, suggestions, and proposals of prominent, though not necessarily profound, conservative writers and thinkers. It is all very well to listen to President Reagan or one of the administration's leaders or a conservative governor talk about the need for fiscal austerity or to hear the President relate, as he often does, the story of the "Welfare Queen" of Chicago and how she defrauded the government. But it is important to know who influences the president and his appointees, as well as other office holders, on urban questions, and how and why they are so influential. Plausible answers to these questions are suggested by examining the works of those conservative thinkers who have devoted the most attention to the cities and their problems. They are Edward C. Banfield, William F. Buckley, Jr., Milton Friedman, Irving Kristol, and Ayn Rand.

These five have been chosen not only for the quantity of their output, but also because they have established themselves as prominent writers in a way that guarantees a certain measure of influence. Each has also established a discernible popular following through book sales; through positions as editors, reviewers, television personalities, and public figures; and through academic and journalistic affiliations. Their popular followings, composed of what may be assumed to be an active and relatively well-informed group of people, make it likely that the ideas of these five will gain acceptance and take form as public policy in urban America. Four of the five (all save Rand) have had the ear of the White House in Republican administrations, serving as official or unofficial advisers on urban, economic, international, social welfare, or other policy questions. Rand's influence has been more indirect: she has a faithful following and elite-level readership which includes government officials or ex-officials, such as Alan Greenspan, Martin Anderson, and David Stockman.[5] Two of these five, Buckley and Rand, can be described as cult figures. Friedman probably also fits this description, especially since winning the Nobel Prize and starring in his own television series. All five are authors of widely read and highly acclaimed books. Three of the five—Banfield, Friedman, and Kristol—have had distinguished academic careers and university affiliations. The five have credentials as novelists, journalists, economists, or political scientists. They represent disparate approaches in studying the city. In varying degrees, all of them have demonstrated originality and creativity in their views on urban issues and problems. All five, however, have constructed approaches and policy solutions that dovetail at enough points to delineate a conservative view of the city. Their attitudes towards authority, for example, show a marked emphasis upon its maintenance and its desirability even in the face of factors and considerations that cast severe doubts upon the fairness of certain regimes.

It is important to point out that all five of the writers' works should be considered eminently political; they should be viewed thus in order to achieve the goals of this study and to describe the essence of their works. These writings are meant to be political acts, and so it does not matter whether their contributions are considered fiction, sociology, journalism, economics, or political science. Not one of the five can be regarded as a "trimmer," willing to soften words or tone or to hedge on issues to accommodate a given political climate. This is one of the great advantages of using them as sources. Not one of the five is a politician, at least in the traditional sense of the term, but all five have sought to be overtly political in setting out their views. (Although one of these writers, William F. Buckley, Jr., ran for the office of mayor of New York City, this had no "trimming" effect upon him.) On occasion, the views of the five may seem to meld; however, that is to be expected when producing a composite from disparate sources.

The composite picture of the City of the Right which will emerge from this study is based upon a variety of conservative positions. The problem remains, however, of defining conservatism, both in terms of its application to each of the five thinkers and in the broader terms which apply to the composite structure of their views. Logically, there should be little difficulty with the latter if it can be established that each of the thinkers is a conservative. Fortunately, this is a manageable task. Four of the five (again, all except Rand) would agree to such a characterization, and they are accommodating enough to use this term in self-description. The problem of classifying Rand is surmountable; it will be demonstrated that her outlook and policies are at least conservative in implication. To a great extent, then, the five principals of this study offer a conservative portrait of the city by calling themselves, their view

of the city, their policy goals, and their philosophy "conservative."
It is certainly conceivable that some people, who also refer to
themselves as conservatives, may object to the composite City of
the Right and/or any of its components.

It is necessary, of course, to define conservatism within some
comprehensive terms of reference. One of the strongest tendencies
of conservatism, American or European, is the belief in inherent
human inequality. This belief has roots in a variety of sources; for
example, conventions of custom and law, privileges of one social
class when compared to another, inequalities of the natural
abilities of people, or misunderstandings resulting from ethnocentrism. Edmund Burke, a favorite of many American conservative
thinkers, believed that a natural aristocracy arose from a natural
division of labor. People of ability and wealth—and bloodlines—
should therefore be regarded as our naturally-selected leaders.

Natural selection of another kind is found in a second important
influence upon American conservatism, Social Darwinism. Drawing
from Charles Darwin's *Origin of the Species* in the latter half of
the nineteenth century, Social Darwinists applied the "survival
of the fittest" doctrine to America's processes of industrialization,
capital formation, and income distribution. A justification for
inequality was found in biological destiny as interpreted by
economics. In one sense, the concept of Social Darwinism was
nothing new; a variant had been practiced, for example, in ancient
Sparta. Social Darwinist writings had a profound effect upon the
mind of Hitler. And although Social Darwinism is probably less
important than some other influences upon American conservatism—
respect for traditions, religious piety, or the work ethic—it continues
to crop up in many ways. "Biological elites" often wish to
establish sperm banks and maintain that IQ tests are infallible
measures of racially related abilities.

American Populism, the great grass-roots agrarian movement
of the late nineteenth century, has also affected conservatism,
though this seems to be more a matter of style than substance.
As a practical matter, Populism seems to have touched the five
subjects of this work very peripherally, if at all. Irving Kristol,
in fact, loathes the Populist tradition, finding it dangerous,
moblike, and antirepublican.

Tradition is a conservative value. Burke believed that it represented the collective wisdom of the ages and therefore deserved our respect. It appears important to Banfield, Buckley, Friedman, Kristol, and Rand, all of whom praise the American experiment and the vision of the Founders. They also see a solidly based development of wealth through capitalism and its free markets, which are traditions of our history as well as our mythology.

Religion is a part of the American tradition, of course, and these thinkers—with the notable exception of Rand—seem to uphold it as central to our hopes of continuing as a nation. They regard the waning of religious influence in American culture as a catastrophe for our cities as well as for the whole country. Buckley and Kristol are acute articulators of this position. One regards the battles over urban issues as conflicts, in smaller arenas, which reflect the cosmic struggle between atheism and faith. The other feels that the loss of belief in an afterlife is the greatest change of our modern experience and that the dire effects of this are tied to the development of an "urban civilization."

The work ethic has a religious connection. The ethic is sometimes called the "Protestant Ethic" because of historical circumstances, particularly as interpreted by Max Weber. The association of hard work with godliness (a view attributed to the Puritans and others), eventually became secularized during the American experiences of industrialization and the later Western movement. And, as Irving Kristol points out, later immigrants who, knowing perhaps nothing at all about the Puritans, already had incorporated, long ago, the work ethic into their values. One of the legacies of the work ethic, however, is the concomitant view that poverty in America is a sin; it is something that happens only to the lazy or the doltish. The antipathy of conservatives to the guarantees of the welfare state, however minimal these may be, is understandable in light of the sanctified position of the work ethic. It should be recalled, however, that the work ethic was devised in an agrarian era and that an urbanized, technologically advanced economy can create unemployment and hardship of severe proportions. Welfare state measures which provide some protections against the ravages of unemployment, poverty, poor health, or just plain bad luck seem necessary, despite the costs involved and the inefficiencies

produced. Not one of these five thinkers is very concerned
with this view; indeed, all condemn the welfare state. Rand would
dismantle all of it; the other four would leave only a few
skeletal remains.

The welfare state is said to work to the detriment of the free
market system. This system, especially as outlined in Adam Smith's
Wealth of Nations, is greatly admired by American conservatives,
including our five principals. The system is efficient; it has produced
the greatest prosperity the world has ever known; and it has, from
their point of view, served the greatest needs of the greatest
number of people. The "invisible hand" of the market system
promotes not only each person's particular selfish interest; it
also promotes a general good through such mechanisms as price
competition, product quality, and the availability of incentive.[6] We
will see that one of the problems with cities today is that their
policies, and the federal policies that encourage certain responses,
are antimarket. Solutions for this set of circumstances are offered
which, in the main, are intended to revive the market system
and its values by encouraging the free choices open to each
person.

There are immense problems, of course, with any suppositions
about the market economy. First, it is doubtful whether such a
freely competitive system has ever existed except in very limited
times and places. Second, the logic of general welfare based upon
individual greed is not sound. And third, freedom and choice,
it must be admitted, may be enhanced by governmental actions.
Housing, education, or health measures, for example, may be
beneficial in offering opportunities for a better life to some
individuals. This remains so despite the great disdain that
conservatives and, for that matter, many others, hold for government programs today.

A strong belief in progress, not through government but through
the innovations and development of technology, also seems to
surface in conservative writings. The liberating effects and abilities
of technology make it necessary to promote research in private, but
not so much in public, institutions. In addition, the technological
elites must be protected by these institutions and, if necessary,
by public policies, for they help to make the economic system

work. Unleashing the oil companies will bring the energy crisis to an end. Deregulation of transportation systems will promote efficiencies and innovations. Of course, conservatives are not alone in their faith in technology; but some of them—Friedman and Kristol in particular, and most especially Rand—are adamant in supporting it against the advice of some economic planners and environmentalists.

It is not difficult to find students of politics who agree with the elements listed so far as parts of conservatism in America today. Inherent human inequality, some elements of Social Darwinism, tradition, religion, the work ethic, the free market and a belief in technology are all either apparent or latent landmarks in the City of the Right. Many observers and critics may disagree, however, with my next element on the list, namely, the promotion of political orthodoxy, and most importantly, the promotion of political orthodoxy *often to the exclusion of* libertarian considerations. It will be shown that in the case of each one of the City of the Right thinkers, civil liberties receive cavalier treatment and an uncomfortably low priority at too many points.

This list of characteristics of conservatism does not provide a full definition of the term. Like all political terms of consequence, it has a certain amorphous character at times. It must be mentioned that conservatism should be placed within the context of many generally shared values of American political thought. A foremost value is the anti-urbanism of some of the Founding Fathers, Thomas Jefferson in particular, a value which has evolved into an important intellectual current in our history.[7] It can be found today in such varied writers as the hard-headed political scientist, Robert A. Dahl, who suggests an optimal size of 50,000 to 200,000 population for a city in order to achieve the fullest benefits of a public-spirited, participatory democracy, or Theodore Roszak, who feels that the city has taken us away from the values of magic, tribalism, ritual, and the love of nature.[8]

Banfield, Buckley, Friedman, Kristol, and Rand proceed in their analyses from a variety of assumptions. These general formulations of conservatism will be set out and explored. Next, the conservatism of each thinker is applied to the view of the city and its problems. This step serves as a bridge between the topic of conservatism and the urban policies which are the focus of the final section of each chapter. The policy positions are best understood in the light of the conservatism of each thinker and the "urban vision" of each thinker. This urban vision is the integration of the conservative outlook and an urban view that, if one prefers the more exalted term, is actually an urban philosophy or a set of assumptions and attitudes about cities within the constellation of values of each thinker. The policies—or, more precisely, the policies as discovered and understood within the context of conservatism and its approaches to the city—are the ultimate focus of this work, for they will tell us a great deal about what to expect from the City of the Right.

The broad outlines of such policies are probably known, or can be guessed, by any astute observer of the American political scene, but a precise understanding of the policies, the "urban vision," and the conservative premises of these five will go a long way towards explaining the dynamics of the relationships between conservatives and the cities, the attention and support (or nonsupport) given to cities by conservative regimes in Washington, D.C. or in state governments, and realistic expectations for cities in a time when conservatism seems to be going from strength to strength.[9]

It should not be surprising, in the coming months and years, to see the Reagan administration adopting any number of the policies favored by these prominent conservatives. The president has already said that we will be doing things for the cities more cheaply, if we do them at all.[10] He has apparently begun to work on the task of developing the City of the Right.

Notes

1. Eugene Lewis and Frank Anechiarico, *Urban America: Politics and Policy,* 2d. ed. (New York: Holt, Rinehart, and Winston, 1981), p. 250.

2. *Wall Street Journal*, March 10, 1981.

3. Thomas R. Dye and L. Harmon Zeigler, *The Irony of Democracy,* 5th ed. (Monterey, Calif.: Duxbury, 1981), p. 122; Peter Henle, "Exploring the Distribution of Earned Income," *Monthly Labor Review* 95 (December 1972): 16-27.

4. *Gallup Opinion Index*, Report 170 (December 1979), shows that 44 percent of the public places itself "right" of center as opposed to 34 percent who are "left" of center.

5. Buckley, Friedman, and Kristol were all called upon to give advice to the Nixon administration, and all serve as advisers of one sort or another to President Ronald Reagan. Buckley served in the United Nations and in the U.S. Information Service and accompanied Nixon on his historic trip to China. Edward Banfield served the Nixon Administration as Model Cities director. On Ayn Rand's strong indirect influence in Washington, see James Conaway, "Hollywood on the Potomac," *New York Times Book Review*, January 11, 1981, p. 11.

6. See chapter 4.

7. Morton White and Lucia White, *The Intellectual Versus the City: From Thomas Jefferson to Frank Lloyd Wright* (Cambridge, Mass.: Harvard University Press and MIT Press, 1962), especially chapter 2.

8. Theodore Roszak, *Where the Wasteland Ends: Politics and Transcendence in Post-Industrial Society* (Garden City, N.Y.: Doubleday, 1973).

9. Obviously, there are a great many factors and explanations concerning the 1980 presidential and congressional elections other than a tendency towards conservatism, such as voter turnout, disenchantment with President Carter's leadership, corporate spending, regional voting patterns, single-issue voting, etc. But it is a mistake to believe that conservatism is a phenomenon found only in the Republican party, and it is a safe assumption that there is a conservative trend in American political attitudes which, although it was temporarily derailed by Watergate, has been a persistent and growing tendency, especially since 1945.

10. *New York Times,* March 3, 1981.

2

EDWARD C. BANFIELD:
THE UNHEAVENLY CITY

Probably the most controversial books on urban America written in the past two decades are Edward C. Banfield's *The Unheavenly City* and *The Unheavenly City Revisited.*[1] These works alone insure a prominent place for Banfield among conservative commentators on the city, but he has also written a number of other well-known books and articles on the subject.[2] Banfield's conservative approaches to urban policymaking achieve their most acute focus, however, in the *Unheavenly City* books, so they will serve as the primary and nearly exclusive source for this exposition.

Banfield's Conservatism: A Time-Horizon Theory

Banfield claims no special expertise in any particular area of urban policymaking but seeks, instead, to collate vast amounts of information and research findings in order to draw up some general conclusions about the urban condition and possible remedies. His various works reveal no apparent commitment to philosophical "givens." Thus his conservatism appears to arise from what he feels are pragmatic concerns about the American city.

The earlier phases of his career may be inferred to bear on the development of his pragmatic conservatism. Banfield served on the front lines of government policymaking, the "real world" of public administration, before he entered academia. Born in Bloomfield, Connecticut in 1916, Banfield received his Ph.D. in political science from the University of Chicago in 1951. Later, after distinguished associations with such great universities as Chicago, Harvard, and Pennsylvania, Banfield again served in government as Model Cities director for the Nixon administration. Now he is back at Harvard where he can draw upon the extensive research facilities of the Joint Urban Studies Center of Harvard and the Massachusetts Institute of Technology.

Banfield is described by some observers as a "conservative conservative" as opposed to a "neoconservative" such as Irving Kristol, Nathan Glazer, or Daniel P. Moynihan.[3] It seems more to the point to describe him as a "pragmatic conservative," one who will support those policies and approaches that appear to be most likely to work. The pragmatic label must be used carefully, however, for Banfield, while displaying no deep commitment to any philosophical approach, does manage to maintain a great deal of ideological rigidity.

The pragmatism of Banfield's approach to cities and their problems is readily apparent in the second chapter of the *Unheavenly City* books, "The Logic of Metropolitan Growth." The history of urban growth and development is presented in matter-of-fact terms, demonstrating what almost anyone in urban fields of study knows about the typical history of American cities: that poor migrants first settle into crowded tenements in the central sections of cities and later move into better and less-crowded neighborhoods and, even later, take part in the process of suburbanization. Suburban growth in the post-World War II period was accelerated by Federal Housing Administration (FHA) and Veterans Administration (VA) mortgage policies and by highway construction.[4] This standard and fairly noncontroversial description of why and how the cities are beset by the problems they have today has been validated by our own experiences and observations and by a vast number of books and studies on the cities. Anthony Downs, to cite just one example, charts the same process of growth described by Banfield in his landmark work, *Opening Up the Suburbs*.[5] The only difference in Downs's description is his more intensive concentration upon what happens to housing stocks as this growth pattern progresses. More importantly, Downs comes up with a very different set of remedies for the urban condition than those proposed by Banfield.

While Banfield's treatment of this growth process is a standard one, some of the conclusions he derives from this seemingly unpolitical chapter are not. Banfield assumes that this process places great limits on our urban policy choices, especially when income distribution, transportation technology, and population growth patterns are considered. But none of these are immutable forces. Banfield's example of the impact of mortgage policies and highway policies upon suburban development shows the ability of government to make policies which can drastically alter the social and physical environment of the metropolis. In fact, Banfield is self-contradictory on the question of poverty, since he asserts in a later chapter that urban poverty "almost certainly" will be eradicated in the next few decades.[6] Banfield's treatment of urban growth and development also presents it as a validation of a bootstrap-type, upward mobility theme. It is something which happens to all of us as a good and inevitable result of joining the middle class, economically, physically, socially, and above all, culturally. This logic of metropolitan growth also renders hopeless the cause of central city revitalization. The only thing to do with the central city is to escape it as soon as possible. This is one of the more dated aspects of *The Unheavenly City* and of its sequel, which were both written before the onset of the energy crisis and the beginnings, in most large cities, of a number of small middle-and upper-class movements back to the central city. This latter process, which has unfortunately been termed "gentrification," involves single persons, childless couples, and even families.

The growth patterns of cities, then, are important "givens" in Banfield's applications of his conservative thought. Placed against this backdrop is the paramount and certainly most conservative "given" of Banfield's analysis, namely, class, which he defines in terms of the "time horizons" of the individuals in a given class. Some conservatives, of course, have been critical of the use of class as a measure of anything, particularly when it is employed by socialist or Marxist critics of society. Banfield's definition of class, needless to say, has nothing in common with these definitions, though it is hardly less sweeping. The mix of class cultures, he explains, is the determining factor in shaping the character of a city and its problems. The political styles adopted in a given vicinity, housing, crime rate, neighborhood relationships, density of population, income levels, all depend upon the composition of classes in an urban area.[7]

Remedies for the urban condition also rely upon this question of class as defined by Banfield. His definition is not economic, though members of what he calls "the lower class" are poor because of their limited time horizon or "future orientedness." Nor is it a social class in terms of traditional social science literature. It is possible, after all, though it is improbable, he reasons, for a reasonably well-off person to be a "lower class" person of limited time horizon or planning abilities.

Problems arise immediately upon presentation of Banfield's scheme of class. This seems to be the experience of many university teachers of urban politics courses who have used his works as textbooks, and also of many social science critics who have grappled with his concept of class.[8] His definition of class lends itself, whatever his intentions, to time-dishonored approaches to questions of poverty, race, and socioeconomic mobility, and, as will be shown, Banfield himself often slips into the graceless and unproved accusations one has heard charged against blacks since time immemorial.

Banfield uses the time horizon approach to class in his dissection of such urban problems as education, crime, race, transportation, and poverty, and this excursion through the issues leads him to set up some tentative policy prescriptions that are more or less preordained by this approach.[9] The difficulties with Banfield's applications of conservative thought are, all along the way, immense, whether they are analyzed methodologically, economically, socially, politically, or morally.

Banfield's Urban Vision

Banfield's vision of the city and of its problems is based upon what he discerns to be the facts. He assures the reader, in his Preface to *The Unheavenly City*, that he is neither ill tempered nor mean spirited, but instead is well meaning and even a little softhearted. "But facts are facts, however unpleasant, and they have to be faced unblinkingly by anyone who really wants to improve matters in the cities."[10]

Improving matters is the key, for Banfield does not believe that urban America is in crisis, a belief that has long suffused all of his writings. In part, Banfield's calm is based upon what he calls the "integrative forces" which are always at work within urban society, forces which determine that city life is not all conflict and struggle.[11] The interdependence of urban dwellers and urban interest groups ensures, at most times, a measure of community spirit which translates into the meeting of needs. Banfield also rejects the idea of crisis because of the nature of urban problems. We may have traffic congestion, for example, but this can hardly be considered a crisis. And should Banfield be wrong about an urban crisis, he nevertheless believes that the time of real crisis is past; so he begins his second treatise, *The Unheavenly City Revisited*, with a quotation of President Richard M. Nixon of which he apparently approves: "A few years ago we constantly heard that urban America was on the brink of collapse. It was one minute to midnight, we were told. . . . Today. . . the hour of crisis is passed."[12] Certain ironies present themselves in this inauspicious beginning. Perhaps not America, but certainly the White House, came apart the very next year with Nixon's resignation in disgrace. The quoted statement also coincides with a finding reported just a few months earlier, in December 1972, in the *Monthly Labor Review*, which showed that, contrary to recent historical trends, the wealthy of America are getting wealthier while the poor are getting poorer.[13] (Much of Banfield's analysis relies upon the opposite premise.) Finally, the events since Nixon's utterance have shown him to be demonstrably wrong. Bankruptcies have threatened New York, Cleveland, and other cities; the energy crisis has not awaited the development of public transportation and other alternatives; and the maldistribution of wealth has become ever more obvious and has contributed, according to some economists, to our current economic malaise.[14] The Liberty City area of Miami and the city of Chattanooga have festered into open rebellion and chaos, indicating that cities may indeed be faced with another round of riots and disorder. These facts are of course stated with the benefit of hindsight, and it is unfortunate for Banfield that he had no crystal ball at his disposal. It remains the case, all the same, that our experience with political and social institutions, and the various remedies proposed to better them, is informed in various ways; and a comparison of the record with the analyses and recommendations which precede that record is one of the best methods of judging them.

In his second edition, Banfield is distressed that many critics of *The Unheavenly City*, despite his protestations, said or implied that the lower class, as he defined it, was to be equated with the poor and/or the black.[15] A reading of either edition will show that Banfield is surely to blame for this impression as much as his critics. For example, if he did not want to be misunderstood, he should avoid such chapter titles as "Race: Thinking May Make It So" or "Rioting Mainly for Fun and Profit." It is certainly true, as Banfield points out, that he has decried racism and its effects, although one could hope for a more straightforward denunciation of racism than appears in such passages as ". . . even if prejudice is not important causally, it is very important morally." and "It is bad enough to suffer real prejudice, as every Negro does, without having to suffer imaginary prejudice as well.[16]

More to the point, it would seem that Banfield could, for the sake of clarity of purpose if for no other reason, avoid making allusions to heredity and biology as factors which influence the lower class. On page 57 *The Unheavenly City Revisited*, he states that it is "not implausible to conjecture that some genetic factor may influence" lower-class tendencies, even though he goes on to say that time horizon is probably a social, not a biological, product. This is murky enough, but then Banfield moves from murkiness to explicit racism some pages later when he allows excess to intrude upon his analysis:

> . . . racial prejudice enters into every sphere of life. Cultural differences (apart from *class*-cultural differences)—and conceivably even biological ones as well—also account in some degree for the special position of the Negro, as they do for that of every ethnic group.[17]

This racism is distressing; indeed, it makes any further criticisms of Banfield pale by comparison. But Banfield also seems to insist, each time he concedes a point to blacks, that he later must take the point away. Thus he tells us of the impossibility of making comparisons of black assimiliation patterns with those of other groups, a good point since it is intuitively assumed by many observers that the factor of skin color makes comparison of problems of, say, the Irish or other ethnic groups wholly specious. Later, however, he says that physically distinguishing racial characteristics do not stand in the way of acceptance and upward mobility because we can look at American Orientals and their situation and see that this is not so. Therefore Banfield both accepts and then later denies the reality of blacks' assimilation problems.

Even the example of American Orientals is not as apt as it may seem at first blush. Japanese-Americans do have, as Banfield states, higher median family incomes and lower unemployment rates than urban whites or blacks do.[18] That Japanese-Americans have been economically assimilative over recent years is apparently true, but it is questionable whether one, especially in the light of a host of cultural values and factors, can hold up one minority group as an example to another. And, to look at the matter in light of all the relevant facts, Japanese-American assimilationist tendencies have not always proved to work to their advantage. World War II saw them placed into concentration camps, and it did not seem to matter, from the standpoint of the authorities, whether they were assimilative or not.

No less telling is Banfield's inaccurate insistence that Mexican-Americans are a recent immigrant group.[19] They may be newcomers in some cities, although they have been present in significant numbers in some Midwest cities since the years immediately following World War II. In California, Texas, and some other states, of course, there are some families whose roots in those parts of America go back to the seventeenth century. They might be surprised to find themselves regarded as new arrivals. This kind of gaffe is inexcusable when it is becoming increasingly important to understand the needs and aspirations of this large, and often urban-centered, group.

It is risky to one's analysis, no doubt, to belabor so many points to advance the single point that Banfield has little cause to complain that his vision of urban America, as set out in *The Unheavenly City*, does not sit well with a great many people. The second edition is also full of distressing lapses, assertions made without an empirical foundation, and, as shown above, occasional departures into overt racism.

Banfield is well aware of the lack of an empirical base for his thesis of classes based upon time horizon, or "future-orientedness." In the Preface to the second edition, he states his hope that his class scheme will eventually achieve empirical verification.[20] The only evidence available to date is that the thesis—or, more correctly, the hypothesis—does not bear up under scrutiny. James F. Sheffield, Jr., and John E. Stanga, Jr., both of Wichita State University, ran an empirical test of three related propositions that undergird Banfield's hypothesis: 1) variations in time-perspectives are sufficient to allow classification of a national sample of respondents into various social classes; 2) such variations relate to differences in sociopolitical attitudes, values, and behaviors; and 3) the time-horizon theory has more explanatory power in terms of such attitudes, values, and behaviors than conventional conceptualizations of class.[21] Their findings showed little empirical support for the time-horizon theory of social class. Virtually no meaningful associations could be correlated with various social and political behaviors, no classification scheme could be developed, and the explanatory ability of the time-horizon theory was shown to be markedly inferior to more conventional definitions and indicators of class.[22] The entire work of the *Unheavenly City* books rests, therefore, upon the slender reed of Banfield's hope that at some time in the future his assertions can be verified. In another sense, then, Banfield has a time-horizon problem of his own. Myth, as will be shown, is a strong force with conservative analysts of the city. But Banfield's conjectures, he says, are in accord with the facts and, in any event, "conjecture unsupported, or slightly supported, by facts are the stuff of which social policies must always mainly be made."[23]

Like William F. Buckley, Jr., Ayn Rand, and other conservatives, Banfield spends a great deal of time worrying about the inadequacies of certain unsatisfactory people, people who collect welfare checks, guzzle beer, watch television, and engage in behavior considered bizarre by middle-class standards but routine by their own standards. He notes that these people are irresponsible to say the least. They do not mind filth and squalor; they do not perform even the simplest repairs needed in their homes; they are careless and often given to vandalism; and they do not mind inadequacies in public facilities, such as hospitals, parks, schools, or libraries.[24] They are wife-beating hooligans who prefer the freedom from routines and the whim of spontaneous violence to the security of square meals and good educations for their children. Most importantly, according to Banfield, they lack future-orientedness.

No one, of course, can approve of this litany of bad conduct; but it is more than passing strange that Banfield has not noticed that this same kind of conduct is the grist of gossip magazines and society columns that feature many foibles of the well-to-do. Bizarre behavior is not limited to any particular economic or social class, and, more to the point, future-orientedness does not appear to be the exclusive concern of middle and upper classes. There is, indeed, some rather strong evidence that a lack of future-orientation characterizes the conduct of all sorts of people today.[25] The late 1970s and the 1980s to date clearly show, for example, a decrease in savings, an increase in consumer debt, and a consumer-spending level so high that it has driven the economy away from an expected recession for several years. If most Americans do not save any, or much, of their incomes, it seems unfair to expect the less affluent to do so. And if eccentric behavior is found in one socioeconomic stratum, it should be expected in others. It is a dubious brand of social science that asserts that the evidence, "such as it is," confirms that the lower class hates steady work because it requires a discipline and prefers poverty without work over a more prosperous existence with work.[26] But the evidence, such as it is indeed, lies with Sheffield and Stenga, who have found that Banfield's category of lower class is of no apparent empirical import.

Banfield may be overlooking other factors that explain such behavior when it occurs in what he calls the lower class. He does not consider the effects of hopelessness, a feeling that pervades the families and homes of poverty-stricken Americans.

Hopelessness and alienation undoubtedly encourage behavior oriented towards the short term, and there is empirical evidence to support this.[27] Banfield, in short, may be overlooking the fact that *future-orientedness requires a future.*

It is also important to bear in mind that the poor usually face multiple problems of health, housing, employment, debt, sanitation, education, and unequal access to public services, and thus their frustrations should be considered in the light of those burdens. It is also possible that the perception of the inadequacies of the lower class is a problem originating in Banfield himself. This Harvard scholar is, after all, a middle-class person with middle-class values who is prescribing conduct for people who may not share those values. This does not mean we must tolerate behaviors which go beyond the bounds of generally agreed-upon standards of morality, but it does mean that we must be careful in our judgments to take account of the causes of anomie and alienation. Some of these circumstances could undoubtedly be solved by money; and some of them may not be serious problems, but merely "problems" wrought by the employment of standards that are either impossible to meet or are perhaps completely meaningless.

Just how large is this problem of the improvident and irresponsible poor? In one sense it is not a problem at all since poverty will almost certainly disappear in a few decades, if we are to accept Banfield's word. In another sense, it is not a problem at all, since Banfield tells us that there will always be the poor.[28] But perhaps the most important measure of the question of the improvident and irresponsible poor is found in the fact that welfare agencies seldom find more than a very tiny percentage of recipients whose conduct calls for close regulation through methods such as issuing chits or script for certain purchases in lieu of a welfare check.

Poverty is seen as a relative, rather than an absolute, problem according to Banfield, and therein lies much of our troublesome perception of it. Irving Kristol has shown, says Banfield, that for nearly a century all studies in all countries have concluded that a third, a fourth, or a fifth of the nation in question is below the poverty line. By definition, then, some percentage is always poor as long as the poverty line is redefined upward.[29] Banfield takes this occasion to fall into some rather foolish forms of deduction. Using Kristol's lead on the matter of the poverty line, he states that a "police brutality line" probably also exists in which perhaps one-fifth of all police actions are arbitrarily said to be always brutal. Fortunately, Banfield does not go on to belabor this particular point, but he asserts that, to a great extent, the problems of the city will always be assumed to be of crisis proportions or, at the very least, unsatisfactorily resolved. This is because expectations are ever-rising and performance cannot keep pace with them.[30] Perhaps there was some truth to this when Banfield wrote his books, but today urban expectations have been lowered in keeping with the shrinking commitments of Washington, D.C. under both Presidents Reagan and Carter, and of state and local governments. It is dubious whether performance ever improved very much in recent years, however, and it is safe to say that none of it has meant much to the urban poor. Since 1972 at least, they have seen their standard of living decline in relative terms, and over the past few years, double-digit inflation has caused a decline in absolute terms as well. Incidentally, the Kristol-Banfield view leaves out the salient facts surrounding the establishment of a "poverty threshhold" in this country, a process which included *lowering* the standard of what constitutes poverty for budgetary reasons.[31]

The Kristol-Banfield example, then, is not very useful nor meaningful, though it is comendable that we typically show some measure of concern for the bottom fourth or fifth of the income brackets. The goals of Banfield and Kristol, moreover, are quite different than the goals of those who concentrate their concern on lower-income levels, for neither seeks to attenuate the ravages of inequality. It is wrong, in fact, to call attention to income differences, says Banfield, because the effect is to engender and strengthen feelings of relative deprivation.[32] The parallels are very strong at this point with Buckley, Rand, and Kristol in eschewing equality and, at the same time, worrying about stirring up a jacquerie. They indicate that one of the worst things to do for the poor is to tell them how bad off they are; they would not know, it seems, if they were not told.

In Banfield's treatment, the problem of poverty finds its own solution in the future-orientedness of individuals. If far-sighted persons are poor, they shall not remain so; if, on the other hand, they have a limited time horizon or none at all, they shall remain poor and their condition is not amenable to social or policy solutions. Banfield has concocted a new remedy for the poor: do nothing at all for them, for they are better off being poor because there is less margin for the irresponsibilities of booze, dope, the dog races, and other excesses.[33] One of Banfield's critics holds that instead of giving us a racist point of view, he has given us something new which is equally pernicious:

> . . . the logical status of Banfield's concept of class comes to be the equivalent to that of race: the thought and behavior of members of a class, as with members of a race, are unrelated to the nature of the society. Just as racist dogma focuses on the fixed biological constitution of man as the source of behavior, so Banfield's class concept directs attention to the relatively immutable 'inward' traits of individuals. Banfield's formulation is thereby to be seen as a species of conceptual alchemy. . . .

> A traditional function of race has been to justify and defend inequality and domination. But race has fallen on hard times, and as a result Banfield's formulation comes to seem attractive to the kinds of minds who would earlier have been drawn to race. His 'class' converts an idea antagonistic to the meaning and implications of race to the political and ideological ends served by the latter.[34]

This may well be the effect of Banfield's nonempirical classification of people into future-oriented and non-future-oriented, and it is certainly possible that this serves as a substitute for racism. It should not be forgotten, however, that Banfield has also displayed racism of the traditional kind in his texts. In fairness, it should be reiterated that Banfield admits that racism exists and is a problem; but he downplays its importance and believes that many of the "misfortunes" (his term) visited upon blacks are misperceived as racial in origin.[35]

The horizonless lower class envisioned by Banfield is described as "preconventional" in its morality, meaning that its actions are influenced not so much by conscience but by what individuals can get away with.[36] But what does this mean? Perhaps the crucial difference between the classes is the financial ability to hire a good lawyer, because surely some future-oriented people must be criminals as well. This preconventional morality sounds like an apt description of many of the administration officials with whom Banfield was associated—Richard Nixon, Spiro Agnew, John Mitchell, H. R. Haldemen, John Ehrlichman, G. Gordon Liddy, all of whom, incidentally, take a hard line on crime issues. Banfield claims that there is a need to inculcate a respect for authority in the lower class. He believes that, in the 1960s, American youths were given the impression that the wrongs blacks suffered justified their breaking the law.[37] One can only conjecture the kind of example created by officials of the Nixon administration, but the events of Watergate post-date Banfield's analysis.

Banfield's chapters on crime and rioting not only show his support for respect for authority, but also his demand that authority be used to suppress crime and the opportunity for it. On its face this appears reasonable enough, but respect must be earned by the law and order establishment as much as by anyone else, especially against a backdrop of official crime, a questionable war effort, and discrimination. Respect for authority cannot be mandated merely because authority exists. ("The law is the law is the law.")

Two other observations are in order concerning Banfield's approach to crime. He advocates daily cash payments by employers in the hope that this provision of ready cash will prevent crimes by any lower-class people who are merely seeking instant gratification.[38] The feasibility of this proposal is doubtful. In those jobs, often called "day work," in which such a system exists, there is notorious exploitation. Safety and work standards are either violated or the employer is exempted from them, and the pay is almost always less than a living wage.[39] To promote the furtherance of such systems and arrangements is highly undesirable from a social point of view. Banfield also seeks to promote measures that he believes will have a deterrent effect upon crime by increasing the probabilities of punishment.[40] This is hardly surprising, since it fits well with Banfield's other attitudes and with the attitudes of the other leading conservatives who are subjects of this study. Whatever the merits may be to this approach, Banfield has allowed himself to be confronted with a logical problem: how can people who have little or no future orientation, people who cannot plan past the next hour or two, be expected to respond to the law with calculations based on probabilities? Are we to expect that people with virtually no planning ability are simultaneously endowed with the talent of making serious (and sometimes intricate) guesstimates about whether or not they will receive a certain kind of punishment for a certain kind of crime? Banfield needs to return to the drawing boards on this one.

Despite President Nixon's calm appraisal of urban America quoted at the outset of Banfield's second edition, he is full of fear of urban disorder. For at least another twenty years or so, he says, there will be enough potential troublemakers in the cities to produce frequent "rampage-forays" as well as some riots. And the media, especially television, will be responsible for some of this disorder if they are not careful. In an interesting section on the effects of television, Banfield implies that the nondiscerning lower classes, who do not have enought sense to plan for the future, nevertheless will have very acute perceptions when they watch television, which will lead them to adopt riot techniques.[41] Banfield uses bitter invective on this topic and considers even legal demonstrations undesirable under the circumstances. This is because such events, acted out by middle-class students and others in conformity with their Judeo-Christian traditions and Puritan ethics, will have a ripple effect: "No doubt most of the blood spilled by the middle and upper classes will be steer's blood carried for the purpose in plastic containers. The effect on the lower classes of this sort of behavior by the upper classes may be incendiary, however."[42] This interpretation of urban disorder may be satisfying to some, but the complex cause-and-effect mechanisms of urban alienation are not always so obvious and are particularly difficult to measure. Even from a purely intuitive standpoint, it appears to be a search for less obvious causes of anomie than those which various studies and reports have shown are important.

Banfield has painted a bleak urban scene, one which may accord with the leaders of the Reagan administration. The fate of the cities of America is, according to this view, in the hands of those with a primitive cast of mind who, with no concern for the consequences, are willing to riot on very short notice for the slightest of reasons.[43]

Banfield's Urban Policies

What does Banfield propose to do about this? Where does a pragmatic sort of conservatism lead in terms of urban public policy? The *Unheavenly City* is full of varied proposals. Some are made in all seriousness, and there is a long list of proposals in his penultimate chapter labelled as a set of "feasible" measures considered, unfortunately, "unacceptable." A number of them overlap, so that it is assumed that they must be taken seriously. These include intensification of the police presence in high-crime areas, reducing the school-leaving age, abolishing the minimum wage, some regulation of television coverage of possibly incendiary events, and establishment of fixed standards for measuring poverty.[44]

Banfield shows no concern for downtown redevelopment, viewing it essentially as a concern for the comfort, convenience, and business advantage of the relatively prosperous. He also sees no great crisis in questions of urban aesthetics or urban design. Though there is little urban visual pleasure, this lack is neither an individual nor a social disaster. He believes that the revenue problem of the cities arises, to a great extent, from the way in which jurisdictional boundaries are drawn; unlike William F. Buckley, Jr., who wishes to keep the cities and suburbs separate, Banfield hints at his support for metropolitan reorganization and consolidation schemes. Though his works are dated in the discussion of transportation policy, Banfield exhibits no particular concern with this area and seems content to maintain the current car-centered systems. He admits that racial segregation patterns persist in housing and are deliberately maintained, but he seems to make no connection between this problem and the issue of jurisdictional boundaries.[45] It seems fairly certain that the maintenance of segregation is one of the motives for the lack of integration of urban and suburban governments.

Looking at the issue of employment, Banfield assures the reader that "it is not true that unskilled workers cannot get jobs."[46] But things must be getting worse, for in his first edition Banfield said instead that "there is not much unemployment among unskilled workers." Another notable change that occurred between the two editions is interesting. The earlier work says that "Negro incomes are growing as fast as white, but while Negroes are increasingly well-off *absolutely*, the gap remains nearly constant in *relative* terms." (These are Banfield's italics.)[47] This claim is simply omitted in the *Revisited* edition, because it is no longer true. The gap has widened considerably in recent years, but Banfield has proved himself so polemical, so eager to make his case, that he is unwilling to note this important fact of changed circumstances.

Banfield, like many conservatives, asserts that the minimum wage causes unemployment. He would abolish it and let wages for unskilled workers fall to their natural level, however low that may be. He does not consider the "cost of a job" question (baby-sitting, bus fares, and so on), nor the question of human dignity. What, after all, would a pay cut do for the psyche of ghetto workers? He insists that labor should not be paid more than it is worth and that the minimum wage law does not cause an employer to raise wages.[48] This policy proposal raises the question of what the Wage-and-Hour Division of the U.S. Department of Labor has been doing all of these years. The Division's files show case after case in which an employer, having violated the law by paying less than the minimum, later conformed with the law (albeit under duress) and paid the wage without laying off anyone. One of Banfield's major concerns is that the minimum wage hits unskilled workers and young workers harder than anyone else, creating a reluctance in employers to hire them at $3.10 per hour or whatever future increases in the law may require. Most recently the case against the minimum wage for youth, and the minimum wage generally, seems to have fallen upon hard times. Senator Orrin Hatch, a Republican from Utah who has long been a proponent of antiminimum wage and "youth-differential" legislation, has decided to abandon such efforts upon taking over as chairman of the Senate Labor Committee. An aide to the senator offered the useful explanation that Hatch "would be a fool to say he's wedded to an idea where we don't have hard economic evidence of its job-creation ability" for the unemployed.[49]

While he would abolish the minimum wage and while he frets about paying labor more than it is worth, Banfield would offer tax exemptions and other concessions to induce businesses and plants to stay in the city or to return to it from the suburbs. Banfield admits that making this approach work would require very large subsidies and concessions.[50] He agrees with the extensive literature showing that city governments rarely can offer subsidies large enough to have much effect, and then goes on to say that this is just as well, anyway, since cities must establish themselves as centers for services and exchange rather than as production centers.

To his credit, Banfield condemns suburban zoning ordinances which have the effect of excluding low-income people. Any interferences with the right of workers to live where they please, whether it be the suburbs or the inner city, is regarded as contributing to unemployment. Ultimately, however, Banfield despairs of finding solutions to the problem of unemployment when he says that some will remain unemployed even when good jobs are offered to everyone. And Banfield may well be right; but this has never been tried.

Like the four other thinkers in this book, Banfield has a hearty dislike for the free public school system. He feels that schools are inhabited, to a great extent, by students who do not wish to be there, and so he would turn them out at age fourteen with an education compacted to do in nine years what it has heretofore done in twelve.

He emphasizes the attainment of marketable skills for those who will drop out (or will be dropped out), and a well-rounded education for a much smaller percentage of students than is presently given this opportunity. After all, Banfield insists, "It is not feasible . . . for every child to get a high school education as distinguished from a high school diploma (social and perhaps even biological reality prevent. . . . ")[53] Once again, we have an allusion gratuitously tacked on to his analysis illustrating Banfield's Social Darwinist tendencies.

Banfield's list of feasible, but unacceptable, policy proposals must be handled charily by anyone seeking to understand him and his work. Banfield states that the purpose of this list is to provide a take-off point for a discussion of the reasons why such recommendations must be rendered pointless.[54] But if they are worth discussing at all, as Banfield indicates they are, then should not these recommendations be considered as serious proposals? Some of them are mere reiterations of points made in his earlier chapters so must be considered to have some measure of validity. One might also ask, if these measures are unacceptable, why bring them up at all? Incidentally, Banfield does not say to whom these proposals are unacceptable, although it is assumed that he is specifying a majority or well-organized minority of the general public.

It is risky to criticize Banfield on these proposals, because they are presented so equivocally. On the other hand, friendly conservative observers take these proposals seriously and laud them enthusiastically, including the First Amendment violations directed at the press and electronic media. The magazine of the Young Americans for Freedom, *New Guard*, says that this "list of a dozen proposals . . . provides a sound framework on which to build an urban conservative strategy."[55] Whatever Banfield may require of his readers in terms of discernment and prudence, it is obvious that many professed adherents of conservatism are likely to take his proposals to heart. Certainly this has been the experience of any number of teachers of urban politics courses who have used the *Unheavenly City* books as texts.[56]

Although there is probably no way out of the confusion on the degree of emphasis placed on these proposals, it would be a remission to ignore them. The list is strategically placed in the penultimate chapter of each of the *Unheavenly City* books, and all but one item on the list appeared in both books. The singular exception is the first item, which appears only in the *Revisited* volume. The list:

1. Assure to all equal access to polling places, courts, and job, housing, and other markets.
2. Avoid rhetoric tending to raise expectations to unreasonable and unrealizable levels, which encourage the individual to think that society, rather than himself, is responsible for his troubles, and which exaggerate the seriousness of social problems and the possibility of finding solutions.
3. If it is feasible to do so (the question of feasibility is here subsumed under an already-stated question of feasibility, making it redundant) gear fiscal policy towards an unemployment rate of only 3 percent; at the same time, abolish the minimum wage, stop overpaying low-skilled public employees harassing low-wage employers; and offer wage supplements in the form of scholarships to give valuable on-the-job training to unskilled youths.
4. Compact twelve years of schooling now offered into nine and reduce the school-leaving age to fourteen.
5. Describe poverty in terms of a fixed standard of hardship rather than in terms of relative deprivation.
6. Offer intensive birth-control guidance to the incompetent poor.
7. Pay problem families (a designation some would presumably wish to resist) to send their children to day nurseries offering programs designed to immerse them in the culture of the middle class.
8. Work out insurance and police practices to promote reasonable precautions for potential victims of crime.
9. Intensify police patrols in high crime areas; give police "stop and frisk" and other extraordinary powers and compensate suspects who are found innocent for the period of confinement in which they awaited their trials.
10. Speed up the trial and justice processes.
11. "Abridge to an appropriate degree" the freedom of those who are likely to commit crimes. This dangerous idea, set out

elsewhere in the two books, includes confinement to small towns of persons who are considered likely to commit crimes according to social indicators and behavior patterns.

12. Make it clear that those who incite to riot will be severely punished.

13. Prohibit live coverage of riots and incidents likely to provoke them.[57]

This last would presumably include the results of court proceedings, which are considered to be the flash points of the 1980 riots in Miami and Chattanooga.

However seriously these proposals are to be taken, they surely reveal the general attitudes and positions of Banfield, and they epitomize the tone and substance of the *Unheavenly City* books. The stress upon authority and upon tightening it, the anthropologically unsound attachment to, and preference for, one culture over another, and the more than occasional indifference to the plight of minorities and of the poor are all abundantly clear. The bleak picture painted and the policy prescriptions presented create less of a sense of urgency than one might reasonably expect in the charged atmosphere of urban America in the 1980s. This is because Banfield relies, ultimately, upon the expansion of the American economic pie to solve most of the problems:

> *The Unheavenly City* is oriented to the needs of a policy-maker who is finally admonished not to be too active. Banfield recommends to his notice the beneficial consequences of such 'accidental forces' as 'economic growth'—a modern secular version of 'the divine hand' that used to produce the harmonious society.[58]

Banfield believes that his thesis of future orientation, then, is in some ways less important than economic growth and its graphic urban form which he calls the logic of metropolitan growth. It amounts to a dated, melting-pot view, a view that is dangerous because it encourages fecklessness, ethnocentrism, and inaction.

That humankind can overcome urban problems and dilemmas is, as Banfield asserts, highly problematical. But we must look for "solutions," in part because we are trapped into this approach by the burdens of our Western social philosophy and in part because there is nothing else we can choose to do which offers any hope.

Notes

1. Edward C. Banfield, *The Unheavenly City* (Boston: Little, Brown, 1970); Edward C. Banfield, *The Unheavenly City Revisited* (Boston: Little, Brown, 1974).

2. Banfield's other works include: *Urban Government: A Reader in Administration and Politics*, which he edited (New York: Free Press, 1969); *Big City Politics* (New York: Random House, 1965); *Politics, Planning, and the Public Interest*, with Martin Meyerson (Glencoe, Ill.: Free Press of Glencoe, 1955); *Government and Housing in Metropolitan Areas*, with Morton Grodzins (New York: McGraw-Hill, 1958); *City Politics*, with James Q. Wilson, a Reagan adviser on crime and urban issues (Cambridge: Harvard University Press, 1963); *Boston: The Job Ahead*, with Martin Meyerson (Cambridge, Mass.: Harvard University Press, 1966).

3. Michael Harrington, "The Welfare State and the Neoconservative Critics," in *The New Conservatives: A Critique From the Left*, ed. by Lewis A. Coser and Irving Howe (New York: New American Library, 1973), p. 33.

4. Banfield, *The Unheavenly City Revisited*, p. 32.

5. Anthony Downs, *Opening Up the Suburbs* (New Haven: Yale University Press, 1973).

6. Banfield, *The Unheavenly City Revisited*, pp. 44, 131. Banfield, of course, does allow for the possibility of change in urban growth patterns. Land uses may be different in the future than they are today, and technology is also expected to impose change.

7. Banfield, *Unheavenly City Revisited*, pp. 73-74.

8. Ibid. Banfield provides a bibliography of reviews and reactions to his first edition in Appendix B, pp. 291-92.

9. Ibid., pp. 269-70.

10. This preface appears in both editions; see *Unheavenly City Revisited*, p. xi.

11. Banfield and Wilson, *City Politics*, p. 47.

12. Banfield, *Unheavenly City Revisited*, p. 1.

13. Peter Henle, "Exploring the Distribution of Earned Income," *Monthly Labor Review* 95 (December 1972): 16-27.

14. Lester C. Thurow, *The Zero-Sum Society: Distribution and the Possibilities of Economic Change* (New York: Basic Books, 1980).

15. Ibid., *Unheavenly City Revisited,* p. ix.

16. Banfield, *Unheavenly City Revisited,* pp. 98, 99.

17. Ibid., p. 84.

18. Ibid., pp. 19, 79.

19. Ibid., p. 78.

20. Ibid., p. vii.

21. James F. Sheffield, Jr., and John E. Stenga, Jr., "Banfield's Concept of Class: An Empirical Test," *American Politics Quarterly* 5 (April 1977): 237-50.

22. Ibid., p. 248.

23. Banfield, *Unheavenly City Revisited,* p. ix.

24. Ibid., pp. 65-66, 72.

25. Lewis A. Coser, "Introduction," in *The New Conservatives: A Critique From the Left*, p. 7.

26. Banfield, *Unheavenly City Revisited,* p. 139.

27. Murray Hausknecht, "Caliban's Abode," in *The New Conservatives,* pp. 203-4.

28. Banfield, *Unheavenly City Revisited,* pp. 131, 143, Also, see the rebuttal of this point by former Cleveland Mayor Carl Stokes in the collection of articles on Banfield in *Social Science Quarterly* 51 (March 1971).

29. Banfield, *Unheavenly City Revisited,* p. 22.

30. Ibid., p. 23.

31. Dorothy B. James, *Poverty, Politics and Change* (Englewood Cliffs, N.J.: Prentice-Hall, 1973), describes both the difficulty of acceptance of the idea of helping the poor within the confines of what she calls "the liberal tradition" and the great variety of machinations which took place when it was finally decided to establish an official "poverty line." Also, see note 13.

32. Banfield, *Unheavenly City Revisited*, p. 141.

33. Ibid., p. 143.

34. Hausknecht, "Caliban's Abode," p. 204.

35. For example, see Banfield, *Unheavenly City Revisited*, pp. 79, 84. It is interesting to compare Banfield's use of the term "misfortune" with the ironic way Bertolt Brecht uses it in his various poems and plays.

36. Ibid., pp. 184-85.

37. Ibid., p. 195.

38. Ibid., pp. 186, 192-94, 198.

39. I am more than willing to testify, from personal experience, that exploitation occurs on a regular basis among "day work" employers and agencies.

40. Banfield, *Unheavenly City Revisited*, p. 200.

41. Ibid., pp. 229, 232.

42. Ibid., p. 233.

43. Like many other scholars who discuss urban riots, Banfield talks about the "Watts riot" in Southern California in 1965; but any perusal of a "riot map," such as those provided by the newspapers or the McCone Commission, will show that it was indeed a *Los Angeles* riot. To call it the "Watts riot," which only designates its origin, can lead to an underestimation of its significance.

44. Banfield, *Unheavenly City Revisited*, pp. 269-70.

45. Ibid., pp. 6, 8, 121.

46. Ibid., p. 103.

47. Ibid., pp. 86, 91.

48. Ibid., p. 111; also, see pp. 108, 118.

49. *Wall Street Journal*, November 28, 1980.

50. Banfield, *Unheavenly City Revisited,* pp. 119-20; the latest studies refuting the tax incentives offered by various states as effective in attracting businesses and industry are described in the *Wall Street Journal*, July 1, 1980.

51. Banfield, *Unheavenly City Revisited,* p. 120.

52. Ibid., pp. 121, 234.

53. See chapter 7 and the education proposal on p. 269; also, p. 260.

54. Ibid, pp. vii, 260.

55. Bill George, "A Case for the City," *New Guard* 11 (January/ February 1972): 27.

56. This includes my own experience; any number of students take the Banfield proposals to heart with great enthusiasm or, at least, with little reluctance.

57. Banfield, *Unheavenly City Revisited*, pp. 269-70.

58. Hausknecht, "Caliban's Abode," p. 206.

3

WILLIAM F. BUCKLEY, JR.:
GOD AND MAN IN THE CITY

William F. Buckley, Jr., believes in "the absolute rule of the City of God and the subjugation of the City of Man." [1]

William F. Buckley, Jr., must inevitably grace any list of prominent conservative thinkers in America today. To millions, he is "Mr. Conservative," the person most closely identified with that kind of philosophy and with conservatism as a political movement. He is a particularly appropriate source for consideration of the urban applications of conservative thought and policy, for he has written volumes of material on the subject and, moreover, he was challenged and compelled to think about cities when he ran for mayor of New York in 1965. Most importantly, he lives and writes in the urban—perhaps one should say super-urban—milieu of that great city; this mere fact of location has enabled him to take full advantage of the foibles, stupidities, and well-exposed follies of the political, literary, cultural, and communications elites of New York whom he regards as the liberal opposition.

Buckley's Traditional Conservatism

Buckley's conservatism is frequently articulated and restated in his columns, lectures, editorials, and television appearances. It has an amorphous and imprecise quality which may be partially explained by his tendency to focus upon the issue of the moment. Anyone who reviews the prolific output of the past three decades must employ a fragment here and a piece there to put together a coherent picture of his philosophy. But a pattern does emerge, and the imprecision (or just plain sloppy thinking) of a particular moment becomes relatively unimportant. Fitting together these bits of puzzles does not necessarily erase the common view of Buckley that seems to hold sway in New York intellectual circles: that he is an adventuresome, interesting, and irritating man of both passion and charm who, at the same time, is self-contradictory and quite willing to establish principles in one case that may not be applied later in a similar set of circumstances, and that he is an old-fashioned thinker who likes to be outrageous, humorous, and sly.

The conservatism of Buckley is supported by his beliefs in religion, patriotism, economic freedom, and tradition. His conservatism is further guided by what he feels is a sense of political realism and, to a marked degree, by his aesthetic preferences.

The aesthetic is particularly important in Buckley's case, for it goes beyond his love of Bach or sailboats. It touches, most of all, his love of language. Perhaps this is paradoxical for a television personality, but Buckley remains, preeminently, a person of the print medium. In his more pedantic moods, he will revive an archaic term or phrase just for the sheer joy of displaying it (and of displaying himself). This practice may vex some people, but it is perfectly legitimate and, for that matter, he may be doing our badly battered language a service in this age of "you know," "like," and other pathetic attempts to reach for a way to describe the most elementary thoughts or events. How one wishes, for example, for a Buckley to break the monotony of the simple-minded and vulgar Nixon White House transcripts! Buckley's appreciation of language places him in a category apart from those venal, ignorant men who, it must be remembered, he gladly helped to put into power. Buckley also recognizes that an emphasis upon, and a cultivation of, our language is one of the best ways to confound anti-libertarians of all stripes who seek to impose a Newspeak conformity upon us.

Love of language does not of itself ensure writing quality or the quality of political dialogue. Some of Buckley's work is very bad indeed, full of inappropriate metaphors and inelegant syntax. He is notorious for interrupting his quotations of others with petulant and often needless parenthetical references to the temperament or morals of the quoted person. Buckley is committed to quality and often refers to it in his columns, but his most severe critics charge that he should begin to answer his own call for quality control after thirty years of ceaseless production. If he wants quality, they ask, where is his? Or is his call for quality a convenient cover for sharp practice in political debate?

Debate is another of his passions. No one questions his debating skill, his expert parry and thrust, his relish for repartee, his eye for vulnerability. But is Buckley's "Firing Line" program for the Public Broadcasting Service (PBS) really a good testing ground for these talents? How many can "win" a debate against a skillful antagonist who is both moderator and agenda-setter, cutting you off when you start to make a telling point and dwelling upon your weakest (or apparently weakest) lines of argument? His choice of opponents is also questionable; many of them have intellectually and logically sound ideas but are not used to scoring debate points, while others do not even have a well-grounded understanding of their own point of view. This makes the program a bore, at least by the time of the fiftieth dicing and pulping. It is often alleged that Buckley is *merely* a debater and that his concentration upon making points and upon hammering his opponents is debilitating to his thought processes and narrows his intellectual scope. Whether this is true or not, everyone knows that Buckley likes to "win," and that debate is perhaps his greatest pleasure.[2]

The charge that Buckley's debating style is self-debilitating rings true, because even though it is possible, through hard work, to delineate the major characteristics and values of Buckley's conservative outlook, it is impossible to find any depth, much buttressing, or any great emphasis upon corroborative statements or evidence beyond a superficial understanding of politics and of people. Perhaps this is why, in most circles and at most levels, Buckley simply is not taken seriously. The common light-hearted response to him tends, in turn, to make those who are genuinely horrified by his statements to apper as Chicken Little types who see evil and danger in every nook and cranny of the political Right.

A different but equally important response to Buckley, which often crops up in conversations or in print, is that he is really a tongue-in-cheek political commentator who, although he will not say so, does not intend to be taken seriously. His writings are just the American version of *Punch* or perhaps more subtle burlesques than those of Art Buchwald. Certainly this view must be considered in analyzing William Buckley's critique of American urban problems and concerns. And if these assertions are correct, Buckley should be placed in a category with William S. Gilbert and Thomas Nast (along with Art Buchwald) rather than with conservative commentators on urban America such as Milton Friedman, Edward Banfield, Irving Kristol, and the totally humorless Ayn Rand. There is no reason to lend any credence to such assertions, however. Buckley's writings are very serious, to the point that one often wishes he was not. His choice of topics, his approach to them, and his prescriptions are clear enough; in fact, they are often bald and gruesomely plain. Here are some examples:

> It seems to me that the United States has lagged behind in developing the art of repression. There are now enough eyewitness reports to the activities of the mob—in Watts, Harlem, Detroit, Cleveland, Cincinnati, New Haven, Newark— to justify the generality that we are suffering much more from violence and disorder than we are suffering from inadequate opportunities for dissent.[3]

> The Fifth Amendment (as currently interpreted) should be repealed. Procedures should adapt to the criterion: Did he do it? Procedures should adapt to the goal of speedier justice.[4]

> Under certain circumstances dictatorship is best. I'm interested in human freedom and the kind of government that

maximizes it. I think I would have more freedom under
Franco, for instance, than I would have had under the
Spanish Republic.[5]

Democracy has no eschatology; no vision, no fulfillment, no
point of arrival. Neither does academic freedom. Both are
merely instruments. . . .[6]

Buckley has never indicated that he does not want to be taken
seriously. He believes, quite fervently, that examining the
record is the way to research facts, statements, conclusions and
commitments. Therefore, this analysis will not be burdened with
asking whether each of his statements is serious or merely facetious,
for this inhibits political discussion. Buckley's statements must be
taken at face value unless and until it is learned that analysis and
interpretation of them must be based upon other criteria. He has
never indicated that it should be otherwise; he has written and
spoken "for the record" (which, incidentally, is the title of one of
the regular features of his *National Review* magazine), and he must
be interpreted and judged on that record. Unfortunately, his
record has seldom been analyzed, even though Buckley is really
too influential to be ignored. He has managed, as a result, to
go unchallenged while spreading some of the most errant nonsense
and claptrap imaginable.

The liberal guests on Buckley's television shows often begin
with odes to their host. The ode usually takes the form, as it
did on one occasion with Richard Goodwin, of setting out a
general objection to the thought of conservatives coming to power,
but, if they do, then let it be Buckley, they say. At least, it is
assumed, we will then have conservative governance tempered by
good sense and humane considerations. It is fitting to point out
that no such ode will be found in this study. This author hoped
that conservative governance could have been avoided, but since
conservatives did gain control in 1980, let us hope that Buckley's
voice will be ignored.

Buckley's public career covers almost the entire post-World War
II period. It begins with the publication of *God and Man at Yale*,

his first book, in 1951.[7] The book caused some ripples in academia, but, more importantly, it had a profound effect upon conservatism as a national movement. It is not, of course, useful as a sourcebook on urban applications of conservative thought since it is devoted to Buckley's view of Yale as he perceived it at the time—a place in the hands of liberal professors who owed more than they realized to the university's benefactors. What they taught and wrote was at odds with the interests of those who support and provide the Yale Endowment, and this clearly should not be permitted, he felt. Education, after all, says Buckley, is "largely a matter of indoctrination any way you look at it," and, since this is the case, the only question is what kind of indoctrination is to be programmed into the university. The cry of academic freedom, which someone might raise against this assumption, is, as shown above, a mere shibboleth which, according to Buckley, contravenes both morality and common sense.[8]

Born in New York City on November 24, 1925, Buckley has lived most of his life in the City and in Connecticut, though it is clear from his writings and temperament that he prefers the latter. It could be said that he is a squire in Connecticut and a scribe in the City. New York is the headquarters of the *National Review* magazine, which he edits and writes since he founded it in 1955. The *Review* (circulation around 100,000) remains the focus, and perhaps the catalyst, of the various enterprises of Buckley's career—his appearances on the national lecture circuit, his syndicated newspaper column, and his "Firing Line" television program. He also appears in a variety of other print and electronic media and occasionally advises politicians and even presidents. Buckley is also the founder and guru of two unique political organizations, Young Americans for Freedom and the Conservative Party of New York State.

His mayoral race in 1965 had some of the features of a lark. He did not expect to win but sought only to ruin the chances of the Republican candidate, John V. Lindsay, who won anyway. Buckley's expectations had not been high: when asked by reporters what he would do if elected, he answered he would first demand a recount.[9] Any disappointment Buckley may have felt was more than compensated, however, by the Conservative party election victory in the U.S. Senate race of his brother, James, in 1970. Even though James lost his seat to Democrat (and prominent neo-Conservative) Daniel Patrick Moynihan six years later, his victory must stand as a significant accomplishment for the Buckleys and for the Conservative party.[10]

William Buckley was also an occasional adviser to President Nixon, accompanying him on his famous mission to China. In 1964, he was a close confidant of Republican presidential nominee Barry Goldwater, and a warm relationship has persisted through the years. Earlier, in 1951 and 1952, Buckley was connected to the Central Intelligence Agency (CIA) and to the U.S. Information Agency.[11]

Buckley's active political life and his prodigious writing output are the work of a conservative zealot who, however formally educated at Yale and earlier schools, learned his basic political, social, economic, and religious lessons from his independent, wildcatting, oil-rich father. His religion is Roman Catholic of a peculiarly orthodox kind, one which has impelled William Buckley, Jr., sitting in his New York editorial office, to worry and write about the orthodoxy of some popes and some Church innovations, such as the replacement of the Latin mass. Most of Buckley's writings are concerned with political matters, of course, but he is informed in all of the issues which gain his attention by his belief, set out in his first book, *God and Man at Yale*, that "the duel between Christianity and atheism is the most important in the world. I further believe that the struggle between individualism and collectivism is the same struggle reproduced at another level."[12] It should be clear, then, that in approaching the problems of urban life, Buckley is using the standards of the City of God, perhaps as set down by Augustine, to judge the City of Man. And conservatism, his political standard by which he measures almost everything, would be unthinkable without its religious base. Conservatism, he says, is "a movement in which religion plays a vital role."[13]

But faith, by itself, is not enough, for the components of patriotism, economic freedom as he defines it, and tradition are necessary to round out the true conservative and, for that matter, the whole of life. Even with all of these characteristics of its fundamental nature included, conservatism is neither for the blind sloganeer nor for the lazy mind, according to Buckley. Conservatives, after all, are not omniscient, and their premises, while admirable, will not automatically provide political analysis nor ensure against inconsistency. Buckley exhorts them to inform themselves, stay on top of events, and recognize the foibles and weaknesses not only in the positions of the opposition but also in conservative stances. Conservatism must be reasonable, related to rational processes of the mind; the absence of such mental exercises will cause debates to be lost.[14]

At the same time patriotism, even superpatriotism, is vital to the conservative armory. This is a repetitive theme in Buckley's writings.[15] It is also a terrible and convenient bludgeon to use occasionally against the political enemy, and Buckley's devotion to a variety of rightist witch-hunters, such as Senator Joseph McCarthy, is well established.[16] He probably quotes Whittaker Chambers, the great spy-fingerer of the 1940s, more than anyone else. Buckley's credentials have remained strong with the John Birch Society and other fringe units of rightist cadres because his flag-waving has been both steady and robust over the years.[17]

Economic freedom, as Buckley defines it, is just as important as patriotism for the maintenance of the American and the conservative way of life. In a sense Buckley manages to straddle the two main currents of conservative thought in post-1945 America—the superpatriotism, witch-hunting and support for big defense budgets that have been obvious since the early 1950s and the economic individualism and libertarianism that were dominant values before the war and have remained important ever since. Economic freedom requires as little government interference with the free market as possible, he argues, for the passage of any bills, any laws, or any appropriations is a dilution of our liberties.[18] Free market economics are praised in heaven, he continues; conversely, it is wrong to try to tinker with the natural order of things in order to create something approximating heaven on earth.[19] This is neither possible nor just. Quoting Eric Voegelin, one of his favorite political philosophers, Buckley has stated on many occasions that we must not immanentize the eschaton. We must leave heavenly

matters to heaven and not try to create utopias here on earth.[20]
Economic freedom is basic; other freedoms, in fact, flow from it:

> It is a part of the conservative intuition that economic
> freedom is the most precious temporal freedom, for the reason
> that it alone gives to each one of us . . . sovereignty—and
> over that part of existence in which by far the most choices
> have in fact to be made, and in which it is possible to
> make choices, involving oneself, without damage to other
> people. And for the further reason that without economic
> freedom, political and other freedoms are likely to be taken
> from us.[21]

Critics could argue that this definition of economic freedom is
defective on several grounds. It does not seem so obvious to
the urban poor, for example, that the choices made in the exercise
of this freedom are always "without damage to other people."
Certain investments by those making these choices—in the production
of various consumer rip-offs, in exploitative slumlord ventures, in
public projects (such as highways) which are promoted by selfish
interests whose investment "choice" is to oil the forces of assent—are
socially and economically harmful to the body politic as a whole
and to certain groups in particular (for example, labor, the poor,
minorities, women, consumers).

Nor is "choice" so broad in application for most of us;
Buckley's use of the term brings to mind Herbert Marcuse's
critique of modern capitalist society, in which he states that
many of the "choices" we are allowed to make are meaningless:
which toaster to buy, which kind of automobile style we prefer
(there are more than 50,000 combinations of make-model-body
style-color-upholstery fabric), or what television channel to watch.
These kinds of "choices" only create the illusion of qualitative
election about the kind of life we wish to lead.[22]

Tradition is the last vital element in Buckley's conservatism.
Although never fully explained, Buckley makes no secret of his
admiration for philosophers who uphold tradition as a value in
itself. Voegelin is one, Edmund Burke is another, and among

Buckley's contemporaries, Russell Kirk is preeminent in this role. But tradition is a slippery criterion to apply, and so Buckley makes it appear that, to a great extent, he merely means that he wishes to maintain the status quo:

> Conservatism is the tacit acknowledgment that all that is finally important in human experience is behind us; that the crucial explorations have been undertaken, and that it is given to man to know what are the great truths that emerged from them. Whatever is to come cannot outweigh the importance to man of what has gone before.[23]

The call to "tradition" is therefore Buckley's most earnest demand on behalf of a cause, an issue stance, or sometimes, just an attitude that he argues upon the rest of us. The trouble is that almost anyone can find a tradition that is suitable for his or her purposes. The Industrial Workers of the World, the Chartists, and the Spartacus rebellion could all be considered part of a tradition, for instance. Therefore, Buckley uses "tradition" in a more specific and limited sense than the above passage would indicate. He means that the tradition which has finally established certain people (including himself) in positions of influence, wealth, and power should not be tampered with; other traditions can be damned. This still makes "tradition" a broad principle, or set of principles, to apply, and he has used it to decry all sorts of proposals, including, for example, a law banning discrimination in state-supported schools.[24] Traditionally, he argued, such proposals have never been applied. Traditionally, we have not treated blacks or other minorities, women, or the poor, as equals, so why, he asks, should we do so now?

Realism, according to Buckley, is one of the attributes of conservatism. It is not a value like religion, patriotism, economic freedom, or tradition, but it is a characteristic of conservatism that it is grounded upon the political realities of the world.[25] Above all, conservatism is a set of political principles which are attainable in this world. Immanentization is a practice, even a sin of the political Left. Conservatism, working from such "givens" as tradition and economic freedom, seeks to meet people where they *are* in their everyday lives, where they are politically touched, moved and bitten. Socialists describe utopias while conservatives work out mortgage payments. Liberals devise grand plans for day-care centers and tinker with the economy to fight unemployment while conservatives meet their payrolls. Academics, at places like Yale, work in an ivory-tower ambience while conservatives *know*, almost instinctively, that the public abhors busing, abortion, feminism, gun control, and tinkering with free market forces. But realism, like tradition, is tricky; anyone can lay claim to it, even those who supposedly work in ivory towers. And no word has ever been misused more than "realism." We know which side in this country, for example, argued for "realism" in Vietnam, just as we know that politically "realistic" solutions are invariably those which are bottled in the vessels of cynicism.[26] But even in the restricted sense in which Buckley uses it, "realism" is found lacking in many of his proposals, as well it might in those of any political writer, ideologue, or politician.

Politics is also a matter of temperament as much as it is of ideology, and Buckley claims that if there is such a thing as a conservative temperament, he does not possess it.[27] Perhaps he means by this that he finds himself unable to adjust to the ways of some of the quieter, more aloof Establishment people in this country, such as the older-wealth families of the East. Perhaps Buckley imagines that his father's rough, pioneering, oil exploration background has rubbed off on him to some extent.

He further states that his brand of conservatism eschews violence, but he is prone to talk about the use of it.[28]

> Now we are experimenting, or so the word leaks out from ingenious laboratories, with all kinds of new devices, some of them having . . . the distinctive virtue of contributing a little ignominy to the situation. My favorite is a form of glue, which I would most willingly shower down upon . . . an aggregation of sit-ins cluttering up the public corridor of an administrative building. The glue in question takes many hours to remove, and during those hours the sit-ins are literally glued together, in a state of *Gemutlichkeit* that goes much further than anything they had contemplated. Another

is a form of soap, banana-peel like, which upsets the balance of even the soberest rioter, making him look positively ridiculous. And who knows, contact with soap might have such an effect on the rioters as water is said to have on witches.[29]

In a more serious vein in the same year Buckley warned that "word should be gently got through to the non-violent avenger Dr. King, that in the unlikely event that he succeeds in mobilizing his legions, they will be most efficiently, indeed most zestfully repressed."[30] Therefore, violence, though eschewed as alien to the political Right, is, after all, all right under certain conditions, and may be righteously cheered from time to time.

Despite what seems, at times, to be a stern rigidity, Buckley willingly parts company with some of the conclusions drawn up by fellow conservatives. For example, he does not agree with Ayn Rand that the marketplace is a moral standard; he recognizes a need for some (though very limited) welfare legislation, and he has occasionally refused to follow a rightist consensus on some issues. Buckley looks most civilized when he is compared with the other writers who appear in *National Review*, for they are the ones who truly make it a squalid little magazine, filled as much with fright as it is with hate. However, Buckley is the editor and should not be allowed to get off lightly; besides, he does write some awful rubbish. The *Review* invariably has an air of self-congratulation about it as the writers and contributors review each other's books, compliment the latest diatribe published by the archconservative Arlington House, and reiterate various eternal truths. Some of the most cherished of these nuggets, from the standpoint of critics, must be the laudatory statements about Richard Nixon, Spiro Agnew, Richard Kleindienst, and others who helped increase the crime rate in the 1970s.[31]

The advertisements in the *National Review* are almost as enlightening as the articles and columns. Tours of South Africa are offered alongside ads for Buckley's books, military books, a guide to "How to Argue and Win," various "sporting firearms," and replicas of infantrymens' belt buckles. A 1978 issue featured an ad shrieking the question, "Will the Communists Pick the Next Pope?" The ads are congruent with, and complement, the magazine's contents, for most of the writers are dour, the kind of gold-hoarding, head-for-the-hills Spenglerians who are always adding a fifth horse to the apocalypse and calling it permissiveness or inflation or diplomatic recognition of China.

It is within this atmosphere that Buckley thinks and works.

Buckley's Urban Vision

At the outset is should be stated that Buckley is not very sympathetic to the city. Urban concerns, he believes, are liberal concerns,[32] Certainly he spends a great deal of his time in New York City, and he was absolutely required to devote himself to urban issues by his mayoral candidacy in 1965. More significantly, he has written a great deal about urban problems and their possible solutions, which makes him a useful source for the analysis of urban applications of conservative thought. But his heart has never seemed to be in it; after working his way, mostly at scratch-the-surface level, through the concerns of law enforcement, budgets and taxes, problems of minorities, parks and recreation, transportation, and myriad other city issues, Buckley often appears to tire. This is most obvious, of course, in his more reckless moments when he draws into the urban arena federal-level issues such as federal labor legislation, federal taxation, and that old favorite bugaboo, internal security. (Yes, there is a Communist menace at the municipal level, too). It is true that federal legislation affects our cities in a host of ways, through revenue-sharing and categorical grants programs, through housing legislation, civil rights laws, and transportation policy, and even (indirectly) through the amounts and types of fiscal support given to the Pentagon budget. It is even fair to say that politics is a seamless whole and that all kinds of considerations, both direct and ephemeral, can be germane at some point in political discussion. In Buckley's case, however, the point is simply that his urban commitment is neither very deep nor long-lasting. Perhaps this is an inherent defect of applying conservative attitudes and solutions to urban problems; perhaps conservatives just simply are not interested enough in the plight of America's cities.

To a great extent this question of commitment is a matter of sensitivity to urban problems. Buckley's rage at the problems of

New York (and rage is precisely what it is) is the rage which often accompanies the first impression of a problem. The rage of the urban war-weary, the people who have been battling the problems for years—mayors, department heads, school officials, teachers, planners, traffic engineers, housing specialists, active citizens and neighborhood leaders—is subdued, but it is rage all the same. The patience and incrementalism learned through years of combat with run-down housing conditions, outmoded service delivery systems, bureaucratic complexity, and worn-out capital equipment, are virtues that sustain a certain level of dedication and competence. These professionals have learned that any possible solutions will be complex and difficult because the problems are complex and difficult. They have also learned that ideologically based approaches are worse than useless because they tend to set up barriers to good administration and problem-solving. Most urban professionals tend to believe, in fact, that ideology at the municipal level of government is irrelevant.

For Buckley, ideology is all-important, and the record shows that he has tended quickly (and often thoughtlessly) to apply conservative analyses and formulas to contexts that often may not accommodate them. One of his principal analytical faults is to take a federal issue and apply it, willy-nilly, to what he considers the local counterpart problem. For example, in dealing with the labor-management relations problems of New York City, he sets out his ideas for a new federal labor law which will be highly restrictive in its effects upon almost anything a union can ordinarily do.[33] But New Yorkers are not helped particularly by being told that what is needed is a new federal law which, almost certainly, will make labor relations more difficult and which, in any event, has no chance of passage. When the motormen are on strike, this kind of recommendation will not get the subways running again. In dealing with city housing crises, Buckley describes his ideal of no federal involvement in housing policy. It is an interesting academic point, perhaps, but the feds *are* involved in housing policy. The vaunted "realism" which Buckley claims as the strength of conservatism seems to have a will-of-the-wisp character.

Whether Buckley is faulted for this or not, it is necessary to look at his view of the state and its role in society in order to understand his vision of the city. His reductionism, that is, his failure to derive approaches and solutions to problems that are appropriate to government at the local level and his insistence upon broad-gauged, federal-level analyses and solutions (there's irony there!) does not in any way vitiate the need to understand his opinions about the state, the meaning of freedom, and the liberty of its citizens. For him, the problems of the municipality and the problems of the larger state merge into a need, at any and every level of government, for the consistent application of the axioms of conservatism. And, before this matter of Buckley's reductionism is dropped, it should be pointed out that conservative rhetoric, including Buckley's, has often told us that the political Right can pride itself upon its concern for local government and local problem-solving, as well as for the consequent need to get away from sending all of our problems to Washington, D.C. for answers. The best conservatives can do, however, is to resort to national-sized shibboleths and reshape them just a little bit in the hope that they will work, albeit in miniaturized form, at the local level. It reveals a certain intellectual bankruptcy.

Buckley questions democracy. For him it has no relevance as an end in itself but only as a means to an end. Democracy, therefore, is merely method, nothing more. According to him, the liberals' strong attachment to it is obsessive and fetishistic, although it is useful to them because, "in an age of relativism one tends to look for flexible devices for measuring *this* morning's truth. Such a device is democracy. . . ."[34] No mere method can lay claim to an intrinsic goodness, and democracy, though it is not necessarily a bad form of government, is also not necessarily nor inevitably a good form of government.[35] It is fair to infer from Buckley's views that the many "choices" he envisions in his version of economic freedom are more important than the kinds of choices offered by the franchise, by representative government, or by a system of alternatives and oppositions in the forms of parties and candidates.[36] The "votes" cast for or against products and services in the marketplace and measured by the forces of supply and demand are considered significant in a way that cannot be matched by the machinations or processes of a political system. And, as we have seen, Buckley believes that wealth ultimately protects individual freedoms far better than any laws or constitutions ever could.

But Buckley does more than question democracy. He has claimed, for example, on any number of occasions, that American government is simply not repressive enough. Repression hardly seems consonant with democratic theory. He also sees no reason why everyone should be permitted to vote. In opposing the Anti-Poll Tax Amendment he argued that it should not be adopted because people would take voting more seriously if they had to pay to vote. Another reason, more to the point, is that

> the Amendment in question is an advance on the proposition that everyone should vote; and I do not believe that everyone should vote . . . [the] alternative . . . is . . . that everyone should have the right to vote whose record or accomplishments more or less suggest that he attaches an importance to the vote that goes beyond his own immediate self-interests.[37]

Buckley has some test in mind to determine voting eligibility and, presumably, the criteria would be drawn up by himself or by people like him. He has never gone as far as the late H. L. Hunt, the Texas oil millionaire, who believed that votes should be allocated by purchase, a million votes for a million dollars or one for one dollar. That would be too crass for Buckley. Either system, Hunt's or Buckley's, would have the virtue of open admission of elite rule, a point now often lost in the manipulative chicanery of electoral politics.[38]

Democracy generally includes protection of minority rights, no matter how small these groups happen to be or how unpopular their cause. Buckley has no qualms about denying protection to certain groups, however. When asked on one occasion about the rights of atheists, he replied, "Well, I'm not particularly concerned about the atheists." He also feels no "obligation to protect the liberties of the Nazi or the Communist or, for that matter, anybody who seeks class legislation or genocide."[39] (Surely Buckley, an advocate of all sorts of class legislation, would lay claim to constitutional protection of *his* rights!)

Like Banfield, Buckley believes in removing certain undesirable people from the city (and from his sight). Chronic welfare recipients should be located, as a part of a "pilot project," somewhere else. Again, constitutional objections and libertarians can be damned, for those who object find it "always useful . . . to discover a Constitutional imperative."[40]

Perhaps Buckley's greatest contempt for democracy is illustrated by the more than mild disdain with which he treats those who employ libertarian arguments against his ideas and programs. Defending his crime stance in his mayoral campaign, Buckley noted that

> there were a few scattered comments to the effect that I desired to modify the Bill of Rights—which, as a matter of fact, are half correct . . . the current movement to fanaticize the Bill of Rights has of course the effect of diminishing certain other provisions of the Bill of Rights.[41]

Buckley's libertarianism, in fact, depends upon the entirely ox-and-gore question of who is persecuting whom. Soviet dissidents receive appropriate sympathy while victims of Franco's Spain or Salazar's Portugal received nary a mention. Perhaps the depth of Buckley's libertarian sensibilities was touched by the Watergate criminals; through much of the period of rule by the "law and order" administration of Richard Nixon, he advised us to proceed with care and a caution that proved to be excessive.[42] On the other hand, he strongly admired the tactics of Mayor Richard J. Daley and his Chicago police in carrying out the sheer brutality of the repression of demonstrators at the 1968 Democratic National Convention.[43] Democracy and libertarianism, then, are of no particular value or importance in Buckley's vision of the city.

These attitudes shed light on Buckley's views about race relations, the major urban social problem of our time. A sympathetic account of the evolution of Buckley's thought on the civil rights issue holds that he went through three phases of development. His first reaction to the *Brown v. Board of Education* integration mandate of the Supreme Court in 1954 was based upon the premise that white Southern culture was superior to that of the black minority. A "clarification" of this view stated that this premise was correct and that "if the majority wills what is socially atavistic, then to thwart the majority may be, though undemocratic, enlightened . . ."[44] In the second phase, while he did not abandon this position altogether, he said that school integration, though perhaps morally desirable, could not be forced upon the South constitutionally because of the Tenth Amendment. Desegregation, according to this argument, was a threat to civil order and to state sovereignty, which had to be the prime considerations. In the third phase he depicted integration as a utopian dream that would fail in the South because it stood at odds with southern tradition. Integration was simply another instance of that immanentization of the eschaton to which liberals and do-gooders are so susceptible. Integration was based solely upon reason, and he believed that "the cult of reason divorced from tradition and faith ends in the brute appeal to force. . . ."[45] Of course, force has always been part and parcel of the brutal racial oppression practiced in the South, but this force apparently had the sanctified characteristic of being traditional.

Many years later, in 1970, Buckley was asked whether he still felt that the mandate of *Brown v. Board of Education* was good law. He answered that it was lousy law and that there were increased grounds for believing that it was also bad sociologically.[46]

However one may choose to sum up these three phases of Buckley's thought on integration and civil rights, along with his later retrospect on the period, there is not much to indicate empathy with the plight of black Americans. A host of statements and writings belie what can only be described as a truly tragic misunderstanding of black hopes and aspirations. His "Reflections on the Assassination of Martin Luther King, " to cite one of Buckley's tackier displays of gracelessness, is a smug and self-satisfied treatise devoted to infantile flag-waving, disregard of the real grievances of blacks, and harsh treatment of blacks and whites for the sin of becoming emotional about the death of their great leader.[47] Dr. King and his methods of non-violent civil disobedience were always a peculiarly sore point with Buckley, so much so that a most far-fetched fantasy was put to ink and paper:

> It is a terrifying thought that, *most likely*, the cretin who leveled his rifle at the head of Martin Luther King may have absorbed the talk so freely available, about the supremacy of the individual conscience, such talk as Martin Luther King, God rest his troubled and compassionate soul, had so widely and so indescriminately made.[48]

Martin Luther King never preached violence, of course, nor should one expect that anyone who hated him enough to kill him would pay much attention to following King's lead. This is surely one of the more outrageous, to say nothing of irrational, pieces Buckley has ever written.

Buckley is not above baldly stating his racist views. Africans will be ready for self-government, he once said, "when they stop eating each other."[49] The Buckleys have been known to send out private correspondence containing such enclosures as a decision by a U.S. District Court in Georgia that black children are "inherently, biologically and genetically inferior to whites, as shown by various tests and testimony," including the witnessed statements proffered by Ernest van den Haag, the *National Review* columnist.[50] The allegation of racial inferiority intrigues Buckley, and he has said that debate can be expected to "continue on the question of whether his [the American black's] gifts are genetically other than those of the Caucasian or only apparently other for reasons of training or environment."[51]

When he is not suggesting the racial inferiority of blacks, Buckley ably demonstrates his abilities in the art of condescension: "The quality and the energy—and the charm—of the black leaders in all of these cities is a major marvel. . . ." After a session with black militants in Watts in May 1969, he asked, "Why don't the oppressed buy shares in Standard Oil?"[52] In truth, Buckley tells us, the demands of blacks are much ado about nothing. We more or less do them a favor by letting them live here in America. After all, he has earnestly pointed out, the average lower-class black in America enjoys a higher living standard then the average upper-class black in a typical African state; the average black has more political power in America than the average black possesses in any black-run state; and blacks enjoy more minority rights in America than any white minority possesses in black-run African states.[53] All of which, of course, is beside the point of achieving equality of treatment in America. Indeed, one could argue that American blacks have enough burdens without being charged with the misfeasances of governments over which they have no control.

The 1965 mayoral campaign was marked by bitter antiblack polemics as Buckley railed against them time and again:

> We cannot help the Negro by adjourning our standards as to what is, and what is not, the proper behavior for human beings. Family irresponsibility; lawlessness; juvenile delin-quency—whatever subtle explanations there may be for the pressures that conduce to them—are nonetheless deplorable, and a matter of urgent social concern.[54]

The conduct of the white majority is exemplary by comparison, he assumed. Columnist Joseph Kraft concluded that Buckley's campaign employed this rhetoric, along with terms such as "crime in the streets," "drug addiction," and "protest demonstrations" in order to make a thinly-veiled appeal to prejudice.[55]

In summary, the Buckley position on race relations, aside from his excursions into gracelessness and crassness (and how can we put aside such vile displays?), is quite untenable in asserting that black demands make much ado about nothing but, at the same time, in stating that black conduct, which is largely irresponsible, is a grave threat. There are deep analytical and moral contradictions, as well as some old-fashioned cart-before-the horse problems, with this position. There is a profound lack of appreciation of the value of culture in an anthropological sense. And there is a chilling racism which is particularly indefensible in the words of a very literate person in late twentieth-century America.

Racial equality is assuredly not a part of Buckley's urban vision. Neither is economic equality. For that matter, neither is equality of opportunity. With respect to the latter, the true test of a reactionary is passed with flying colors; while many people oppose equality as a given or as a value, relatively few Americans are willing to deny equality of opportunity, at least on principle. Buckley is. In a revealing passage in which he decries Yale admissions policies in 1967, he notes that a "son of an alumnus, who goes to private preparatory school, now has less of a chance of getting in than some boy from P.S. 109 somewhere."[56] The old-boy network must be kept humming, and damn the social cost!

Inequality for women also suits him well. Naturally, he opposes the Equal Rights Amendment. He and his fellow *National Review* writers refer to the women's movement as "chicklib." And he positively adores a filthy, sexist poem written for his magazine by William Rickenbacker in a tasteless attempt to burlesque the women's movement.[57]

For the urban poor, he holds out precious little hope. He believes that "poverty, after a certain point, is a subjective rather than an objective condition."[58] Trying to do something about this objective condition is an exercise doomed to failure, just another indulgence in immanentization of the eschaton. When President Lyndon B. Johnson retired from office, Buckley listed the new kinds of programs established in his administration—antipoverty, Head Start, transportation, model cities, rent supplements, voting rights laws, housing, aid to education, Medicaid and Medicare, environmental measures, new food inspection standards, the Job Corps, and so forth—and then asked why so many people are dissatisfied. All of the "splendors of the Great Society . . . left America cold."[59] A trenchant point, though some answers and explanations are available which, more to the point, neither support nor verify his rightist view.

Buckley seems to be quite willing to give up on the poor though he does not believe that their problems stem from their poverty or inequality. He says that the poor are often disorganized; they cannot even be convinced to flush their toilets. If many seem to be hopelessly irresponsible parents, their children should be turned over to charitable organizations, he believes.[60] Above all, the one thing he wants for the poor is to keep them well-separated from the young revolutionary leaders of our society who will tell them how badly off they are and what they should do about it.[61] A favorite belief, not only of Buckley but of many conservatives, is that the grievances of the poor can only be manufactured by those who can best articulate them, thereby stirring up the masses. He does not believe that the grievances may, in fact, be real, and he cannot bring himself to credit the poor with enough intelligence to recognize their own plight. This view informs us, as much as anything does, about the kinds of attitudes that constitute Buckley's vision of the city. It is a view mean-spirited enough to oppose an aid-to-the-handicapped bill on the grounds of budget strain and deficit and the allegation that the Pentagon budget cannot be cut further to accommodate this need. At the same time, he charges that in this era of new earnings records, oil company profits are too low.[62] If less were known about Buckley, the conclusion would be that he seeks, for some quirky reason known only to him, to cast himself as "the heavy" in the great morality play of American politics. This is not the case, of course. Buckley genuinely considers equality not only abhorrent as an ideal, but also impossible to achieve. You simply cannot legislate equality, he often reminds us, and to try to do so is defective policy making.[63]

What of those at the opposite end of the equality scale, the rich? The rich need to be defended, says Buckley, a true class warrior, and he quotes Friedrich Hayek, who has written that if the rich did not exist, they would have to be invented because capital formation, that vital necessity of a free economy, is impossible without the rich. Risk capital can only be provided by the rich (as in America) or by the state (as in Russia). Compare those two countries! Leave the rich alone, Buckley urges; they are evidence of a natural, healthy state of affairs. And don't forget, adds Buckley, they spend money, spreading around their wealth. Too often, their activities, whether good, bad, or philanthropic, are made into political issues. No one, he says, forbids the poor their excesses as a political principle. (No one, perhaps, except Buckley, Banfield, Daniel P. Moynihan, and. . . .) What we should do with the rich, then, is to

> leave them alone, stop scolding every time they give an expensive bash, tell them that the pressures on them will be social and moral and intellectual, not political, not coercive.

Let them alone. They are valuable people. And they have
their own problems. One of them is us. Let's relieve them
of that.[64]

A disingenuous argument; Buckley, after all, is rich by any standard.
The "us" who represent a problem for the rich do not, for
any apparent reason, include him. This circularity should not
confuse anyone; it is just a matter of a simple (indeed, absurdly
simple) apologia for himself, his family, and his class. He is no
different in this than the Rockefellers, the Mellons, or the Pews. It
is only that he is willing to make his points on behalf of his
class and his privileges more stridently and more often, a
nouveau riche characteristic that is not remarkable in a second
generation of oil wealth.

Inequality, then, is a virtue of the good state and of the good
city, he believes, and it is not the function of government, or of
governmental policy, to try to change this natural and healthy
state of affairs. Inequality is the result of tradition, the workings of
a system which is, in his view, characterized by a strong measure
of economic freedom; the values of society, especially religious
values; and, no less important in his eyes, some genetic advantages
and disadvantages. Not only should government refrain from
tinkering with this system; it should also stay out of most areas
of human activity altogether because the private sector—people
and corporations working their wills and carrying out their own
bargaining—is to be preferred because this will maximize the freedom
of all of us.[65]

What is left for government to do? Buckley, like almost all
present-day American conservatives, sees its role as preeminently
one of the Hobbesian function, providing safety and security,
whether on city streets or on a global scale. Conservatives, almost
invariably, argue for big defense budgets. The municipal counterpart, our police forces, are also given a preferential position in
government by conservatives, whether they be the John Birchers
telling us to support our local police or William Buckley playing
up to police groups and law-and-order hard-hats in a mayoral
campaign.[66]

Buckley considers large garrisons of peace forces, with a very
free hand in pursuing their duties, absolutely necessary for the

establishment and maintenance of order. The nature of the threat to this order must be understood if we are to combat it, and Buckley feels (actually, knows) that he understands it. It is absurdly simple to describe: criminals, malcontents, and barbaric mentalities are out there on our streets, doing their dirty work of making a civilized existence impossible for the rest of us. No further explanation is really needed, for Buckley does not care to hear about social causes of crime. Social anomie is not easy to measure, and even if it can be measured and correlated with social conditions, this does not impress Buckley. He occasionally gives readers the impression that he recognizes the complexities of crime; unfortunately, he always backs off from such discussions to resume his call for repression, for doing away with Bill of Rights provisions, and for chastising those who would be empathetic with the criminal, the poor, or the downtrodden.[67] Asked if he would disagree with the assertion that eliminating poverty would eliminate crime, Buckley flippantly said, "I would. Drug abuse and crime both have to do with the state of the ethos; and the ethos is not a function of poverty. Consider Portugal or Ireland: Poor people don't necessarily commit crimes."[68] His choice of Ireland for validation of his point is certainly regrettable, as anyone knows who has followed recent events in that violent country. His choice of prose, "ethos" and the rest of it, is disturbing because it is unneccesarily abstruse. Most unfortunately, Buckley seems determined to rely upon cross-national comparisons of crime statistics in a quite indiscriminate way, assuming that crimes are reported in the same way from country to country. How naive! And, on the house of cards he has built with this answer, he places the weight of his flat, unproved assertion of the nonrelationship between social problems and crime. It's all rather too much.

Buckley's belief in state action is therefore principally a belief that action should be limited to the garrison function. Although this is hardly surprising to even the most casual observer of conservative political rhetoric, it raises the dilemma that Buckley shares with nearly all of his fellow rightists: he wants small government so that there is minimal regulation of business and the economy, minimal (or no) consumer or civil rights protections, minimal (or no) aid to the physically limited, and so forth; but at the same time he wants big government, discretionary government, in the field in which governmental power is most meaningful and most dangerous to liberty. This makes his support of civil liberties, such as it is, appear suspect or at least naive.

Buckley's vision of the city is lacking in any deep commitment to the city itself, faulty from an analytical point of view, defective in its approach to democracy and fundamental questions of civil liberties, uncaring about the poor and racial minorities and, even further, demonstrates a belief in the inferiority of the innate qualities of such people. Blatantly racist at times, condescending, ethnocentric, graceless, and sexist, Buckley revels in inequality and an only occasionally checked power of the police. It is not an attractive vision; surely it is no utopia (but then, Buckley is not one of those immanentizers); and, most interesting of all, it has a certain familiarity about it. It looks like the condition of our cities today. Our cities are, in fact, largely a kind of fulfillment of Buckley's vision; and so one should logically ask why he does not like the cities more than he apparently does.[69] Aren't they undemocratic enough? Aren't they unequal enough in their treatment of people? Better still, aren't they repressive enough? Perhaps not; after all, Buckley has been described as a man of "extraordinary inhumanity."[70]

Buckley's Urban Policies

Buckley's vision of the city translates, mostly in predictable ways, into policy positions. Some of these positions were enunciated as early as the mid-1960s, but few of them have been adopted. The 1965 mayoral campaign was a particularly productive time for his urban proposals, but additions occur from time to time. Some proposals, such as a "Buckley Bikeway" for New York City, are genuinely attractive to people of all shades of political opinion. Most of his proposals, however, seem to share two characteristics: first, they fit snugly into modern-day conservative dogmas, and, second, they tend to be solutions that city governments, in the normal course of procedures and events within our federal system, do not have the power to impose. Quite often, in fact, Buckley's answers to urban problems contain the ironic requirement of federal action.

There is also a decided tendency to avoid the mundane and presumably unexciting issues that do not yield easily to pat ideological panaceas, but which, quite often, are at the heart of municipal governance and at the center of citizen concern. Foremost among issues in this category are the provision and delivery of services, efficiency of administration, bureacratic reorganization, and decision-making systems, including citizen and neighborhood involvement. Some of these concerns, especially the latter, may slightly postdate the sources necessary to discern Buckley's urban policy positions, but this is a minor factor since, in the main, Buckley is simply not interested in writing about these issues.

Education policy is a good starting point, since the views held by any political writer on education help to illuminate the policy stances taken on a whole range of issues. It has already been shown that Buckley believes that school integration, whether in the North or South, whether aimed at de facto or de jure discrimination, has been an enormous failure.[71] Buckley also believes that education is a matter of indoctrination no matter how one seeks to establish and administer a school system. Schools are not, therefore, neutral. He points out that we know our values, the great truths of life, the Ten Commandments, the American heritage. Tradition, the natural order of things, religion, the economic and political truths that made the United States a great country are a part of the purpose of life, a purpose that is known because it has been told to us and because we can understand it. The aim of educators and of educational institutions is to pass on these truths and the various methods to find and understand them. This will help to inculcate loyalty of students "to the great certitudes of the West...."[72]

Not surprisingly, Buckley values private schools, and in part this is because he believes that God-and-country values are ignored in public schools. He fears that we are headed towards a monopolization of education by the public school system, although recent statistics on school enrollments should assure him that this fear is not borne out by the trends. On several occasions, he has advocated a voucher system to save the private schools, which would permit all parents to send their children to schools of their choice with tax dollar support.[73] Strongly criticized by the teachers' unions and others as a threat to public education, voucher systems are also subject to the charge that they are attempts to subvert the First Amendment's separation of church and state clause. As for that clause, Buckley feels it has been zealously overextended by the Supreme Court's *Everson* and *McCollum* doctrines, which establish a high "wall" of separation, and, for that matter, by Thomas Jefferson upon whom these doctrines are based.[74]

Ideally, as far as Buckley is concerned, the public schools would be weakened by a massive opting-out brought on by the voucher systems. Practically speaking, the public schools are still, in Buckley's eyes, too much involved in the process of preparing students for college. We need to differentiate, very sharply, those who are educable and those who are merely trainable, he says. Vocational training should be emphasized for the latter group, beginning at age fourteen, and an early school-leaving age for these trainees is highly desirable.[75] Again, Buckley is at one with Edward C. Banfield, whose *Unheavenly City* recommends getting the more troublesome students out of school earlier. The schools, in other words, should validate and reinforce class differences. Never mind that the British attempts to do this, with their notorious tracking systems and eleven-plus exams, were immense failures. (The eleven-plus, now abandoned, was a test taken at eleven years of age that determined what kind of a school the English child would attend—a grammar school with its academic emphasis or a secondary modern school with its vocational and "three R's" emphasis. The system was based upon the deliberately falsified findings of Social Darwinist Cyril Burt.) And now it has been well demonstrated that our testing systems, so much a part of this kind of differentiation, are ineffective in measuring or predicting student performance.[76] Certainly, if students wish to drop out of school at a reasonable age because they no longer wish to be formally educated, they should probably be accommodated; but Buckley is not saying this. He would force out some who might wish to remain in school.

As much as possible, Buckley sees a need for inequality in education, both in terms of educational opportunity and in terms of education itself. Public schools should track students, using sifting systems that will render a kind of elite that manages somehow to survive through all of the filters. This will not only aid the middle and upper classes of our society; it will promote and protect a certain standard of quality, and quality is one of Buckley's most frequent and insistent demands. Of course, even Buckley will compromise quality for good and expedient reasons. For example, he believes that academic credit for Reserve Officer Training Corps (ROTC) instruction is commendable.[77]

These are the central features of Buckley's urban education policies. There are some less important points, such as his coolness to the idea of government-subsidized school lunches.[78] After all, he admires Milton Friedman enough to appreciate his axiom that there is no such thing as a free lunch. It is all right, though, to take government subsidies when they are offered. Buckley, for example, went to Yale on the GI Bill.[79]

The issues of poverty and the welfare state clearly describe Buckley's ideological position since his approach to them is largely ideological. It is easy to believe that he is on automatic pilot as he declaims and pontificates on those subjects that he regards as improper concerns of government at the municipal level or at any level. He is not against all welfare measures, but it is impossible to find Buckley waxing enthusiastic about any of them.

Buckley believes, first, that it is most unfortunate that American society has evolved to a point where, he reasons, social welfare, rather than such traditional functions as crime control, has come to hold a priority position.[80] Social welfare threatens economic freedom, says Buckley, though according to critics, this freedom is a sham. In any event, this view reveals Buckley's materialism more than anything else. Economic freedom is the

> freedom, when one works for a barely living wage, to provide unhelped against illness, emergency, and old age; to retrain oneself, when half one's working life is over and the free market has made one's trade obsolete, for a new occupation; to combat the oppressions of large corporations by buying stock in them and taking part in stockholder democracy . . . this [Buckley philosophy] is a philosophy of purely material values, regardless of [its] religious vestments. . . .[81]

A bare and minimal protection against life's vicissitudes is all that Buckley can bring himself to support, and sometimes he cannot support even that. He has said we should investigate Milton Friedman's negative income tax scheme so that, perhaps, some minimal floor can be placed under income.[82] During the Nixon years, however, Buckley found himself, at different times, on both sides on the Family Assistance Plan (FAP) worked out by Daniel P. Moynihan and reluctantly supported by Nixon until he decided to drop the whole idea. The FAP scheme would have provided only $1,600 a year as a guarantee for single incomes, not much money even in 1970. Buckley apparently became loathe to accept any such plans because he believed, quite wrongly, that the United States was rapidly eliminating poverty.[83]

This oil-wealthy Connecticut squire has maintained some confusing and inconsistent postures on poverty when it comes to stating preferences. However, he has never wavered in his condemnation of the poor. He has stated, for example, that it is crucial to distinguish between the "disorganized" poor, those whose life structure and habits make them incorrigible, and the transiently poor, those whose poverty will not persist but, instead, will diminish as they make use of their opportunities for social and economic mobility.[84] He apparently has some preference for the latter; yet he vehemently opposes the chances for mobility of which they may make use, thus increasing the probability that they, too, will join the ranks of the incorrigibly poor. He dislikes the Supreme Court's *Shapiro v. Thompson* decision, for example, even though its invalidation of state residential requirements for welfare recipients has demonstrably made the poor feel less inhibited about moving in order to improve their lot.[85] He is also strongly against immigration, feeling that unemployment and other social problems in the United States are too great for us to cope with under the best of circumstances. Why, then, he asks, should we open our doors to any of the world's poor?[86]

In the final analysis, Buckley's view of social and physical mobility of people depends upon who is moving and upon who is moving whom. He applauds the postwar exodus of white middle-class people from the cities to the suburbs, pointing out that this was the natural thing for them to do under the circumstances.[87] He also finds it worthwhile, à la Edward Banfield, to forcibly deport some of the poor from the city. As a candidate for mayor in 1965, he promoted a project to be employed for this end. (There was no allusion to due process of law.) One critic, exaggerating, said that it was "not unfair for Buckley's opponents to accuse him of wishing to set up deportation and even concentration camps outside the city" for those who had committed the sin of being poor.[88] It can be seen that on a range of issues, Buckley believes that the key patterns of social and physical (and ultimately political) movement must be governed by the well-to-do and the elite of our society.[89] Immigration is vehemently opposed; residential barriers are applauded; movement by the relatively well-off is fine; and enforced movement, even against the will of individuals, is seen as a necessity. The fairest implication to draw from this is that while Buckley condemns people for their poverty, he also opposes opening avenues of opportunity that would give the poor a chance to escape their plight. The old saying, "you can't win for losing," seems apt. There is also—at least there *should* be—civil libertarian and moral questions raised by the enforced immobility or relocation of people. Buckley never addresses these.

There are a few other positions on social welfare and poverty policy held by Buckley that deserve mention. He opposes government-run or -subsidized day care centers because he believes their establishment is a threat to the family.[90] He believes that earnings limitations for Social Security recipients should be lifted.[91]

And he has a curious set of policies on the workings of federalism and the administration of the traditional categorical grants-in-aid programs. He argues that the federal government should not dispense poverty or welfare aid funds to states, such as New York, which have per capita income higher than the national average.[92] Poor people living in better-off states should take up the slack themselves.[93] He is also upset that relatively prosperous New York State receives more from the federal government in various social welfare and grants-in-aid payments than some poorer states receive.[94] This should be no surprise; like the famous car-rental company, New York has traditionally tried harder, and therefore deserves the benefits it obtains. Most of the grants-in-aid and categorical aid programs are established on a matching funds basis to encourage participation in them. This may not always be fair as far as many individuals are concerned, but it is the essence of federalism. If Arizona or Mississippi or some other state wishes for its people to play the "rugged individual" game, the federal government is not likely to do more than establish minimums of assistance. It does make good sense, however, for Washington, D.C. to provide certain incentives for certain policies. Buckley's sympathies for the low-tax, anti-union, poor-services states of the South and West have always been great, but the shift of political and economic power now taking place, much to the advantage of these regions, may eventually make his point moot. These quibbles about the administration of poverty programs and the appropriateness of federal incentives are probably of little substantive concern to the urban poor, who find little to cheer about in Buckley's substantive policy positions.

Buckley regards labor law as a municipal issue; at least, he treated it as such in his mayoral campaign. For the unions, he advocates a great number of "reforms." First of all, he would ban any strikes that extend beyond two weeks.[95] Work rules and procedures, such as the introduction of labor-saving machinery, would never be subject to collective bargaining nor even to consultation. Industry-wide bargaining would also be out, as well as any simultaneous contract expirations within a single industry.[96] In addition, Buckley would apply antitrust laws to unions; labor history has amply demonstrated that this will destroy unions. He wants a bill of rights for management, specifying that strikes are unlawful as conspiracies, thus denying strikes as a civil right. He also urges a national "right-to-work" law to end all "compulsory unionism." Moreover, any company operating at a loss would not be required to bargain with a union until the firm improved its profitability. And, if this combination of "reforms" did not somehow manage to destroy unions (and they would), Buckley asks for a review of the whole question of whether unions should be allowed to exist at all. Naturally, Buckley is in lockstep with Banfield and Friedman in calling for the repeal of minimum wage laws.[97]

In the field of housing, Buckley believes that no government really should be involved at any level. He points out that the urban renewal programs of past decades were often failures that displaced more people than they housed. Housing and urban renewal have been, of course, particularly weak links in the liberal armor. This does not mean that government involvement in housing is necessarily ruinous. England has shown us that a government's broad-scale commitment to housing can go a long way towards meeting a national need; in addition, it cannot be said that all of the programs of the U.S. Department of Housing and Urban Development (HUD) or of the Veterans Administration (VA) have been failures. Buckley and other conservative critics of government housing programs, such as Martin Anderson, cannot be very easily refuted, on the other hand, particularly when the damage to neighborhood integrity and city aesthetics is assessed. The effects of the work of liberal-acquisitive coalitions in city after city have created this blight, and the situation will not be easily rectified.

Buckley's housing program for New York City includes 1) an end to rent control, 2) opting out of all federal urban renewal programs, 3) renovation and modernization of older buildings, 4) encouragement of small, self-contained working and recreational communities, and 5) reduction of housing investment costs by lowering city taxes, denying the monopoly powers of construction unions, and discouraging the flow of migration into the city by establishing residence requirements for welfare.[98]

Transportation is an issue that, to be charitable, Buckley simply does not understand. He was imaginative in coming up with his Buckley Bikeway idea for New York, and it is a pity that it has not been adopted. But his demand that transit systems should pay for themselves (something no other city services do) begs the question of transit economics.[99] The truth is that if so-called economic fares were charged by the public transit industry, then almost no one, save the transit-dependent, would desert their cars to ride the bus or subway. Nor is Buckley correct in saying there is "no obvious reason why Cayuga County apple-pickers need to be taxed in order to subsidize the 5,000,000 New Yorkers who regularly ride the subways."[100] Indeed, there is. Encouraged by lower fares, public transit benefits almost everyone when energy and environmental considerations are tallied. Buckley's major transportation and anticongestion program for New York City included: 1) experimentation, such as a charge on all out-of-state cars coming into the city, 2) exclusive bus lanes in city tunnels, 3) truck deliveries on alternate days, 4) fares to pay the full costs of bus and subway operation, 5) busting the Transport Workers Union, 6) free fares for the very poor, 7) no immunity for diplomatic cars from traffic regulations, 8) an increase in the number of taxi franchises, multiple passengers in cabs, and arrangements for handicapped persons to order cabs by phone, and, 9) the bikeway, which would stretch across Manhattan.[101]

Buckley has had little to say about local government tax structures. He apparently believes that a value-added tax (VAT) would be beneficial for cities to adopt, but it also appears that he has given scant attention to this idea.[102] Support for a local VAT is really a knee-jerk, ideological response to a complex issue. It fits the traditional conservative and Buckley preference for taxes on consumption, which favor the wealthy and encourage savings, and for flat tax rates, which allegedly encourage incentive and have virtually no relationship to the ability to pay. The most tangible benefit of a value-added tax is that it has a proven ability to raise a great deal of revenue. Depending upon how a VAT scheme is drawn up and administered, the general assumption is that a tax is added with each product or service component. In paying the retail price, the consumer also pays for the accumulation of sales taxes with a final levy added for the retailer to collect. Buckley does not spell out how he thinks this would work as a local tax, but part of the revenue-raising advantage of a VAT would be lost if it played only a local role because fewer components and add-on stages would occur in a local situation. A VAT would also place local products at a disadvantage if other cities did not adopt the tax. For a city like New York, which already has competitive disadvantages, the results would be detrimental if not disastrous.

Buckley's national tax plan also includes a provision for flat, rather than graduated, rates, but it has the virtue of simplicity since it would do away with all loopholes and tax concessions.[103] This measure's effect on the cities is difficult to predict, but it is plain that flat rates place the poor, and even middle-income people, at a disadvantage. Buckley claims that the aggregate revenues produced by the wealthy are relatively insignificant: "When will the professors learn that the money doesn't exist up in those high brackets to run a rapid transit system, let alone bring relief to the middle class?"[104] Assuming that he is correct (and one really cannot tell without knowing which income groups he is referring to specifically), there remain the moral questions of ability to pay, equality, and the obligation of each citizen to pay his or her share of the costs of government. But Buckley has no concern for equality and would not uphold the ability to pay as a criterion for tax policy.

Inevitably, crime control, the major function of city government as far as Buckley is concerned, is the policy area in which he is most explicit about what the City of the Right should be like. He strongly favors capital punishment, which, until the most recent New York mayoral election, had generally been regarded as a state-level or national isue. Admitting that no evidence exists to show that capital punishment is a crime deterrent, Buckley believes there is also no evidence that it is not. He also considers capital punishment neither "cruel" nor "unusual," despite the prohibitions established by the Eighth Amendment. It is only unusual because governors and other officials, interfering with the administration of justice, have made it so. It is not cruel because it is neither painful nor undeserved. As for the inequality of it, "The business about the poor and the black suffering excessively from capital punishment is no argument against [it]. . . . It is an argument against the *administration* of justice not against the penalty. . . ."[105] Whatever one may think about capital punishment, it is clear that Buckley, who is willing to assign other-worldliness to his opponents, is neglecting realities in support of an abstract conception of justice. Capital punishment seems to be the least tenable issue upon which to make this mistake.

The crime program he offered as a mayoral candidate had several points in its favor. It provided compensation for witnesses and for indemnification of victims of assaults and other violent crimes. It also called for the hiring of additional policemen and for outfitting them with the latest technology. But with a barbarous thrust out of place in New York or any other city in our supposedly civilized age, the program referred to the "fanaticization" of the Bill of Rights, opposed civilian review boards or any citizen control of police procedures and practices, and sought to pressure judges to stop "criminal-coddling" policies. Buckley would also tighten parole procedures, quarantine all narcotics addicts, promote legislation for more severe punishments of young delinquents, publish the names of juvenile offenders, and establish a system of paid informers.[106] All in all, the program savagely attacked not only crime, but also the very features of constitutional government that have most differentiated America from other societies.

It has been said that Buckley "thinks exactly like a cop."[107] Perhaps not exactly; but this kind of statement receives a measure of validation from his crime program and, even more, from his view of the city as a garrison:

> What a great many people in the United States want to have guns around for is in case they should need to use them for self-protection, in the event of a complete breakdown in law and order. Those who disdain that sentiment should perhaps imagine themselves a) with a gun, and b) without a gun, living with children in a tenement building and spotting an arsonist down the hall. In such contingencies, it is natural to desire speedier means of relief than a telephone call to the American Civil Liberties Union.[108]

Any urban resident, and plenty of others, could also conjure up such tortured visions. Still, it is hoped that they would have a better understanding of the ACLU's purpose and functions. But this armed-to-the-teeth, dog-eat-dog perspective is not healthy for the city or the body politic. No wonder Buckley prefers his Connecticut abode.

Listing and dissecting Buckley's policies returns us, sooner or later, to his vision of the city. It should be reiterated that Buckley is often in the city but is not of it. In the case of this conservative there is not only a profound lack of sympathy but, ultimately, of interest, in the urban condition.

Other policy positions require little elucidation. Buckley believes, incredibly, that cities can deal with their own pollution problems, an unlikely probability given the variety of boundaries set by our federal and state governments. He believes that government services should involve fees as much as possible—tuition, rental fees, admissions, and service fees, among others.[109] This position demonstrates that Buckley can be ahead of his time since this seems to be an increasing trend wrought by tax revolts and the precarious financial positions of many cities.

It could be said that the perspectives of time and place, such as a New York mayoral campaign of 1965, limit the use of Buckley's policy positions on city government. But Buckley himself does not believe this, since he has reproduced these positions in books and in collections of his writings published many years afterwards. The nonadoption of most of his policies leaves them, more or less, in the position of perennial demands. Still, these policy positions provide a good litmus test of the kind of society the City of the Right might become if Buckley's views were to prevail.

Many pictures of the kind of city that would emerge are possible. Early school-leavers, for example, faced with a freer hand given to the police and a work reward of something less than the minimum wage, would probably produce more social anomie than Buckley or anyone would care to see. The value-added tax, and fewer public services (with fees for many of them), and a debilitated school system are also a part of the scheme. Smashed labor unions and rigid, penurious welfare laws could generate increased discontent and despair among the poor and the minorities. Greater enrichment of the wealthy and a general unconcern over inequality round out this spectre. A cruel system of social immobility and even physical immobility, worsening over time because of spiraling inequality, is a good capsule definition of the Buckley version of the City of the Right.

Notes

1. Charles L. Markmann, *The Buckleys: A Family Examined* (New York: William Morow, 1973), p. 123.

2. "All Buckleys have to win," according to Markmann, *The Buckleys*, p. 43.

3. Quoted in *Quotations from Chairman Bill*, David Franke, comp. (New Rochelle, N.Y.: Arlington House, 1970), pp. 241-42.

4. William F. Buckley, Jr., *The Jeweler's Eye* (New York: G. P. Putnam's Sons, 1968, p. 104.

5. Markmann, *The Buckleys*, p. 168.

6. William F. Buckley, Jr., *Up from Liberalism* (New York: McDowell, Obolensky, 1959), p. 111.

7. William F. Buckley, Jr., *God and Man at Yale* (Chicago: Henry Regnery, 1951).

8. Franke, *Quotations from Chairman Bill*, pp. 65, 160.

9. Wiliam F. Buckley, Jr., *The Unmaking of a Mayor* (New York: Viking Press, 1966), p. 5.

10. Of central importance to James Buckley's victory was the fact that it was a three-way race, enabling him to win with less than 39 percent of the vote over Democrat Richard Ottinger and Republican-Liberal incumbent Charles Goodell. In addition, national party leaders such as Nixon and Agnew supported and campaigned for Buckley because Goodell was "liberal" and anti-Vietnam war. James Buckley made a try for a Senate seat from Connecticut in 1980 on the Republican ticket since there is no Conservative party in that state. He was defeated by Christopher Dodd, the Democratic nominee.

11. William F. Buckley, Jr., *Execution Eve—And Other Contemporary Ballads* (New York: G. P. Putnam's Sons, 1975), p. 436.

12. Buckley, *God and Man at Yale*, pp. xii-xiii.

13. Markmann, *The Buckleys*, p. 278.

14. Franke, *Quotations from Chairman Bill*, pp. 51-52.

15. Buckley's comment: "Question. How can I avoid being 'super-patriotic'? Answer. Be superunpatriotic. Next question?" Franke, *Quotations from Chairman Bill*, p. 77.

16. William F. Buckley and L. Brent Bozell, *McCarthy and His Enemies* (Chicago: Henry Regnery, 1954).

17. Markmann, *The Buckleys*, p. 199. Buckley occasionally excoriates the Birchers, however; for example, see Franke, *Quotations from Chairman Bill*, p. 14.

18. Franke, *Quotations from Chairman Bill*, p. 87.

19. William F. Buckley, Jr., "The Road to Serfdom: The Intellectuals and Socialism," in *Essays on Hayek*, ed. by Fritz Machlup (New York: New York University Press, 1976), p. 106.

20. And " . . . consigning that which properly belongs to the end of

life to the temporal order . . . can lead only to grave dissatisfactions'';
William F. Buckley, Jr., *Inveighing We Will Go* (New York: G. P. Putnam's
Sons, 1972), p. 39.

21. Franke, *Quotations from Chairman Bill*, p. 63.

22. Herbert Marcuse, *One-Dimensional Man* (Boston: Beacon Press,
1964).

23. Franke, *Quotations from Chairman Bill*, p. 277.

24. Markmann, *The Buckleys*, p. 80.

25. "Conservatism is the politics of reality," says Buckley; *Inveighing
We Will Go,* p. 37.

26. On the misuse of "realism" as a political term, see Kenneth M.
Dolbeare, "The Coming Struggle for the Soul of the Post-Behavioral
Revolution," in *Power and Community: Dissenting Essays in Political
Science*, ed. by Philip Green and Sanford Levinson (New York: Pantheon,
1970), pp. 85-111.

27. "I feel I qualify spiritually and philosophically as a conservative,
but temperamentally I am not of the breed"; Franke, *Quotations from
Chairman Bill,* p. 16.

28. "One has to go back to the Ku Klux Klan to come up with
violence on the Right. . . ."; William F. Buckley, Jr., *The Governor
Listeth: A Book of Inspired Political Revelations* (New York: Putnam's,
1970), p. 270. This is factually incorrect, as anyone can attest who has the
briefest acquaintance with company-led and -inspired violence against
unions up to the present day, the violence carried out (both officially
and unofficially) against the antiwar movement, and the violence of the
Buckley-inspired "hard hats" against antiwar protestors; see Markmann,
The Buckleys, p. 239.

29. "On the Right," (Buckley's newspaper column), Indianapolis
Star, November 23, 1967.

30. *National Review Bulletin*, August 29, 1967.

31. See almost any issue of the *National Review* published in 1973 and
some published in 1974. The October 1973 firing of Special Prosecutor
Archibald Cox may be a turning point. To his credit, Senator James
Buckley was one of the first Republicans in Congress to call for
Nixon's resignation. Some of the earlier statements of William F. Buckley Jr.
must be embarrassing, however, including his ardent support of Spiro
Agnew and his designation of Richard M. Nixon as a favorite of
conservatives; see *The Governor Listeth*, pp. 47, 61; *Inveighing We Will
Go*, p. 33.

32. Richard Rovere credits Buckley with creation of the concept of
the "Liberal Establishment," and the headquarters of this Establishment
is, of course, New York. Buckley is also devoted to phrases like " . . . the

Simon-pure left-ideologists who breed in New York like jackrabbits. . . .'',
Franke, *Quotations from Chairman Bill,* p. 196.

33. Buckley, *The Governor Listeth,* p. 100; Franke, *Quotations from Chairman Bill,* pp. 152-53.

34. Buckley, *Up from Liberalism,* p. 119.

35. Franke, *Quotations from Chairman Bill,* p. 54.

36. See the discussion covered by note 22.

37. *The Jewelers Eye,* pp. 73-74.

38. Ted Becker and Paul Szep, *Un-Vote for a New America* (Boston: Allyn and Bacon, 1976).

39. Markmann, *The Buckleys,* pp. 252-53.

40. Ibid., p. 243; Franke, *Quotations from Chairman Bill,* p. 6.

41. Buckley, *Unmaking of a Mayor,* p. 197.

42. Buckley, *Execution Eve—and Other Contemporary Ballads,* pp. 108-11.

43. Franke, *Quotations from Chairman Bill,* p. 51.

44. Craig Schiller, *The (Guilty) Conscience of a Conservative* (New Rochelle: Arlington House, 1978), p. 15.

45. Schiller, *(Guilty) Conscience of a Conservative,* p. 17.

46. Ibid., pp. 17-18. Technically, Buckley is wrong in this interview in assigning school busing to the *Brown* decision, though it was a basis for busing decrees.

47. Buckley, *The Governor Listeth,* pp. 21-27.

48. Buckley, *The Jeweler's Eye,* p. 142. Italics added.

49. Markmann, *The Buckleys,* p. 168.

50. Ibid., p. 142.

51. Buckley, *The Governor Listeth,* p. 164.

52. Ibid., p. 160; Markmann, *The Buckleys,* p. 254.

53. Franke, *Quotations from Chairman Bill,* p. 28.

54. Buckley, *Unmaking of a Mayor,* p. 108.

55. Ibid., p. 122.

56. Markmann, *The Buckleys,* p. 264.

57. Ibid., p. 217; Buckley, *Inveighing We Will Go,* pp. 366-67.

58. William F. Buckley, Jr., *Four Reforms—A Guide for the Seventies* (New York: G. P. Putnam's Sons, 1973), p. 21.

59. Buckley, *The Governor Listeth,* pp. 70-71.

60. Ibid., p. 100.

61. Buckley, *The Jeweler's Eye,* pp. 158-59.

62. Buckley, *Execution Eve—And Other Contemporary Ballads,* pp. 264-65, 292.

63. Buckley, *The Jeweler's Eye,* p. 136.

64. Ibid., p. 307.

65. Buckley, *Inveighing We Will Go,* p. 20; Franke, *Quotations from Chairman Bill,* p. 64.

66. Buckley, *Unmaking of a Mayor,* p. 147; Markmann, *The Buckleys,* pp. 239-40.

67. "[The Warren Court has] played fast and loose with the Fifth Amendment by sneaking it into the police station and leaving it in absolute command of the joint"; "On the Right," (Buckley's newspaper column), Indianapolis *Star,* June 18, 1966.

68. Markmann, *The Buckleys,* p. 52.

69. The inequality, the police brutality and other violations of civil rights, the hopelessness of the poor and the black, the emphasis upon crime control at the expense of everything else—all seem to be the natural result of a conservative approach. This also includes the contrast of suburban growth and relative affluence, wrought in part by neglect of the city.

70. This is the opinion of former New York *Post* editor James Wechsler; Markmann, *The Buckleys,* p. 121. Markmann's book contains many quotations of people who know Buckley or are close to him, not all of which are complimentary.

71. "Such emphases as Judge Skelly Wright of Washington, D.C. has put on checkerboard integration are exercises in abstractionist lunacy," Buckley, *The Governor Listeth*, p. 101.

72. Franke, *Quotations from Chairman Bill,* p. 67.

73. Ibid., pp. 66, 231-32; Buckley, *The Governor Listeth*, p. 102.

74. 333 U.S. 203 (1948). These decisions, in turn, were based upon the famous statement, written in a letter by Thomas Jefferson, that there must be a "wall" of separation between church and state in America.

75. Franke, *Quotations from Chairman Bill,* p. 66; but these dropouts would be placed under fairly severe disciplinary restraints in vocational schools; Buckley, *Unmaking of a Mayor*, p. 93.

76. Ralph Nader group's report on the Educational Testing Service bears this out; Fort Wayne *Journal-Gazetter,* January 18, 1980.

77. Buckley, *The Governor Listeth*, p. 344.

78. Buckley, *Execution Eve—And Other Contemporary Ballads*, pp. 285-86.

79. Markmann, *The Buckleys*, p. 55.

80. Buckley, *The Jeweler's Eye,* p. 74.

81. Markmann, *The Buckleys,* p. 158.

82. Buckley, *The Governor Listeth,* p. 99.

83. Buckley, *Inveighing We Will Go*, pp. 45, 284-86.

84. Buckley, *Four Reforms— A Guide for the Seventies*, pp. 27, 29.

85. *Shapiro v. Thompson*, 394 U.S. 16 (1969).

86. Franke, *Quotations from Chairman Bill*, p. 115.

87. Ibid., p. 117.

88. Markmann, *The Buckleys*, p. 240.

89. See Gerald L. Houseman, *The Right of Mobility* (Port Washington, N.Y.: Kennikat, 1979), especially chapters 1-3, 7.

90. Markmann, *The Buckleys*, p. 31.

91. Buckley, *The Governor Listeth*, p. 102.

92. Buckley, *Four Reforms—A Guide for the Seventies*, p. 31.

93. Conservatives, especially those in policymaking or legislative positions and certainly those who are lobbyists, do a lot of buck-passing within the federal system. States, it is argued, should perform functions proposed for the federal level; but at the state level, it will almost invariably be argued that these functions should not be performed at all or, perhaps, that a particular program is such a large enterprise that it can only be performed and financed by Washington.

94. Buckley, *Four Reforms—A Guide for the Seventies*, pp. 32-33.

95. Markmann, *The Buckleys*, p. 300.

96. Franke, *Quotations from Chairman Bill*, pp. 150-51.

97. Ibid., pp. 152-53, 181; Buckley, *The Governor Listeth*, p. 100.

98. Buckley, *The Governor Listeth*, p. 101; Franke, *Quotations from Chairman Bill*, pp. 110-11, 285; Buckley, *Unmaking of a Mayor*, pp. 204-205.

99. Markmann, *The Buckleys*, p. 304.

100. Buckley, *The Governor Listeth*, p. 107.

101. Buckley, *Unmaking of a Mayor*, pp. 220-23.

102. Markmann, *The Buckleys*, p. 244.

103. Buckley, *Four Reforms—A Guide for the Seventies*, pp. 56-57.

104. Buckley, *Execution Eve—And Other Contemporary Ballads*, p. 296.

105. Ibid., p. 401.

106. Buckley, *Unmaking of a Mayor*, pp. 195-97, 217. It is assumed that by now Buckley may, like many people, have changed his mind in favor of a more enlightened attitude towards addicts.

107. Markmann, *The Buckleys*, p. 229.

108. "On the Right," Indianapolis *Star*, June 29, 1968.

109. Buckley, *Unmaking of a Mayor*, pp. 211-12.

4

MILTON FRIEDMAN:
THE MARKET CITY

As the Reagan administration came to power in early 1981, it was bound to have problems with the economy. It was therefore likely to turn to Milton Friedman, the preeminent conservative economist, for advice and guidance. "Friedman," it was predicted, "has great days ahead."[1]

Great days have been the norm for Friedman. A Nobel Prize winner, an acclaimed author and academician, a television star, a renowned conservative with a great following, an adviser to governments in nations as diverse as Britain, Chile, and Israel—what greater glories could be forthcoming? The most generous descriptions and accolades are bestowed upon him. Robert Lekachman, an economist who shares hardly any views with Friedman, calls him "Possibly the most creative economist of his time. . . ."[2] Another commentator looks at Friedman in the light of the publicity, especially the television commercials, that featured Friedman speaking on the property tax issue in a 1978 referendum campaign in California: "a warm, attractive enthusiast, quite unlike most academicians in the zest with which he is willing to carry his argument into the marketplace, but wholly professorial in the confidence he exudes about his point of view."[3]

Matters are sometimes stretched needlessly in order to boost Friedman and his brand of economics. Recently, for example, a letter to the *Wall Street Journal* contained the claim that the late rock star and composer John Lennon had in fact been a "Friedmanite." His vast riches, it was said, could be understood by an economist like Friedman. His impressive creativity could only have borne fruit in a free economic system, the kind of system praised by Friedman. Above all, Lennon's song, "Let It Be," expressed the market forces and, indeed, the market ethic so assiduously promoted and supported by Freidman.[4]

Acclaim for Friedman seemed to rise to a new height after his PBS television series, "Free to Choose," was aired in 1980. He seemed to strike a responsive chord, one that was very much in tune with the times, as he discussed a variety of policy questions, most of which concern urban issues. Although he does not seem to consider himself an urban expert, Friedman has written extensively over the years about such matters as schools, busing, housing, crime, urban renewal and redevelopment, taxation, labor unions, minimum wages, consumerism, and bureacracy. His books, articles, essays, and, most especially, his column in *Newsweek*, have enjoyed a wide readership. *Free to Choose*, the book upon which his television series was based, was on the best-seller lists in 1980. Naturally, Friedman is admired most in conservative circles. Columns of praise are penned in exceedingly flattering prose.[5] Warmth characterizes his relationships with William F. Buckley, Jr. and Irving Kristol. Edward C. Banfield was a faculty colleague at the University of Chicago and in *Free to Choose* is thanked for reading the manuscript.[6] Even Ayn Rand's parsimony in matters of praise has managed to bend, however slightly, in Friedman's direction.

There are critics, of course. There are those who call Friedman the "darling of business," but Friedman likes to point out, "I'm not pro-business. I'm pro-free enterprise."[7] One particularly nasty editorial, commenting upon Friedman's receipt of a Nobel award in 1976, said that Friedman sought to make it obvious that the Scandinavian academicians who picked him were not his professional peers and that "Friedman's graceless arrogance is always a wonder to behold."[8] And even some conservative banking types, such as one anonymous official of the Federal Reserve, are willing to demur on the issue of Friedman's economic competence. When asked whether it would be a good idea to see Friedman transformed from the role of critic into central banker as a kind of experiment, this official responded, "Yes, in a country one square mile in size, somewhere near the middle of Africa."[9] Friedman's ideas may be admirable, according to liberal economist Walter Heller, but they are fated "to work only in heaven."[10] It will be seen that these criticisms are quite insubstantial in comparison with those which are possible, indeed necessary, arguments against some of his dubious urban policy prescriptions.

Milton Friedman was born in New York City on July 31, 1912. He took his bachelor's degree at Rutgers before earning a master's degree at the University of Chicago and a doctorate at Columbia. He worked for a few years as a researcher and as as bureaucrat—yes, as a bureaucrat in the Treasury Department, incredible as that may seem today—before joining the faculty of the University of Chicago in 1946. It was at Chicago that Friedman gained fame as a conservative—more precisely, as a monetarist—brand of economist. He has produced more than a dozen books, most of which deal with the quantity of money in the economy and the need to control the money supply in order to achieve stable prices.[11] However, the books that receive the closest attention in this analysis are the titles most devoted to urban-related policies. They include *Free to Choose, Capitalism and Freedom, There's No Such Thing as a Free Lunch,* and *An Economist's Protest.*[12] In recent years, Friedman, now residing on the West Coast, has been associated with the Hoover Institution of Stanford University, the famous right-wing think tank.[13]

Aside from monetary theory, Friedman is best known as a disciple of Adam Smith's free market economy, as the author of a well-publicized and controversial welfare reform proposal called the "negative income tax," as a foe of trade barriers, and as an opponent of the draft and proponent of the all-volunteer army.[14] Above all, he believes in the American dream, the right of economic and social mobility through individual effort. With all of its limitations, he thinks that the American economic system has made the dream possible and that it is far better than anything else this planet has ever seen:

> My mother came to this country when she was fourteen years old. She worked in a sweatshop as a seamstress, and

it was only because there *was* such a sweatshop in which she could get a job that she was able to come to the U.S. But she didn't stay in the sweatshop and neither did most of the others. It was a way station for them, and a far better one than anything available to them in the old country. And she never thought it was anything else.[15]

He indicates that the only major interference with the dream is government. Government is not the solution for our problems, urban or any other kind. It is *the problem*. It causes inflation by printing too much money, by protecting monopolistic labor unions, by failing to balance budgets, by hampering initiative and capital formation through the tax system, by taxing too heavily, and by overregulating the economy. The record of government in dealing with urban problems is one of miserable failure, according to Friedman, a failure so complete that it is impossible to name a single governmental program developed over recent decades and aimed at poverty, or urban problems, or social welfare, or "reform," that has achieved its objectives.[16]

Fortunately, he can point to an alternative to government far less costly and much more effective: the free market. With its dynamics of free choice, the impersonal pricing system, and capitalist risk-taking, we can hope to arrive at optimal levels of prosperity for all. This system is not only more desirable as well as more efficient; it is absolutely imperative if we are going to remain a free society. If this path is not taken, says the Nobel laureate, we will find ourselves hurtled by bureaucratic rule-making and inflation into a statist society in which the freedom to choose will no longer be a way of life.

Friedman's Free-Market Conservatism

The cornerstone of Friedman's conservatism rests upon two sets of writings, both produced in 1776. One is the Declaration of Independence, authored by Thomas Jefferson. The Declaration demands the noninterference of government in the affairs of people, the role of umpire rather than participant in our lives. It also sets out "life, liberty, and the pursuit of happiness" as the rights of all free people, a phrase obviously inspired by John Locke's "life, liberty, and property."

This Jeffersonian attitude towards government—that which governs best governs least—is complemented by Adam Smith's 1776 treatise, *The Wealth of Nations*. Among other concerns, Smith was appalled at the monopolistic activities of the Mercantilists. His response was a belief in the free market, an economy in which the fetters of neither government nor private monopolists would be tolerated in regulating prices, investment, trade, or production. Friedman, like Smith, believes that both parties to an exchange can and will benefit, so long as their cooperation is voluntary and so long as no external coercion is exercised; likewise, the right to refrain from making an exchange is assumed.[17]

Both Smith and Jefferson recognized that economic freedom is a requisite for political freedom, according to Friedman. They saw combinations of economic and political power as possible, indeed probable, tyranny. The forces of tyranny can be thwarted and dispersed, however, by countervailing economic freedom.[18] And this freedom, which must be perpetually guarded and preserved, rests ultimately upon what Adam Smith called the "invisible hand." This so-called invisible hand is led to promote the private interests and welfare of all because it is actually guided by us all. Each person, seeking his or her own self-interest, is a small cog in the mechanism that guides this invisible hand. This, then, is a system of free choice, a democratic system, if you will, in which the pricing mechanism regulates each and every bargain. If we do not choose to enter into bargains, that is also our right, of course, and this refusal can also have economic effects influencing the "invisible hand." The important point is that there is an intimate connection between economic freedom and political freedom.[19] Voluntary systems of exchange do not guarantee political freedom; but they are a necessary, even though they are not a sufficient, condition for a free society. Freedom to own property is important in this scheme, fulfilling one of the central purposes of a system of free exchange.[20]

Objections present themselves all the way through these assumptions. The world posited by Adam Smith as the best of all possible worlds probably has never existed in many times or places. The "invisible hand" is often manipulated by government or monopolistic corporations. Free trade, an essential ingredient of Smithian economics, is not everyone's cup of tea; we know that many business people who embrace Smith also seek tariff protections, trade preferences, and other favors. The proliferation of subsidies, which seems to be promoted at the behest of most governments, is hardly in line with the precepts of *The Wealth of Nations*. And what about greed? Should we rely upon forces motivated by greed, or which in fact promote it? We should go back to the Declaration of Independence. It also posits the ideal of equality. Where is equality in this dog-eat-dog world of competition and laissez-faire?

Friedman, of course, takes these matters in stride. He knows that business corporations are far from pure. They indulge in monopolistic practices, they seek subsidies from governments, and they do not necessarily enshrine the competitive spirit of capitalism in their hearts. The truth is that they do not really like competition. But the system works, and though it hardly matches the ideals of Smith or Friedman, it is much better than any alternatives of government planning and interference. Besides, the spirit of competition and laissez-faire does surface from time to time. As for greed, it flourishes in all systems. Capitalism restrains greed from doing the harm it might do otherwise by channeling it into the forces of the market. Greed can cause far more harm in statist systems. As for Jefferson's ideals, equality of opportunity, though surely not equality of talents and most certainly not equality of achievements, seems to be a keystone of Friedman's beliefs, as well as an obvious assertion of the Declaration.[21]

These rebuttals do not take some considerations into account, however. First, there seems to be more than a small lack of pragmatism in constantly referring to an economic model that may never have existed and that we know surely does not exist today. Idealism is needed in political discourse and is indispensable to a free society, but let us be clear about it: the *Wealth of Nations* model has very little to do with the actual operations of a modern economy. Next, there is a notable lack of logic, seldom remarked upon, in Smith's (and therefore Friedman's) premise of greed leading to general well-being and liberty. Human experience seems to show that greed begets greed as well as other social evils that have debilitating effects not only on an economy, but on a political system and, most of all, on society itself. Lastly, it is clear that Friedman is historically quite accurate about the intentions of Jefferson and the Founders in their discussions of equality. It is also true, however, that Jefferson, Madison, and other founders regarded slavery as an ongoing part of the political and economic systems of their day, that they did not think of giving the franchise to women, and that those who did not own property were held outside the framework of political respectability. Thus Jefferson's definition of equality can only be answered with a "so what?" It is to be hoped, if not believed, that questions of equality and of political liberty can be answered in ways that fit their times. For his day, Jefferson was undoubtedly libertarian; for our day, the truths about liberty and equality are found, at least in part, by recognizing that we have grown into an industrialized, technologically sophisticated, hopefully more literate and humane, and certainly urbanized society.[22]

All economists seem to have their fixations, and, along with the free market concept itself, Friedman's is the money supply. His economic advice, first, last, and always, seems to embrace "monetarism," the control of the money supply by the Federal Reserve System in order to stem inflation, stabilize the currency, counteract such developments as grossly unbalanced budgets, and provide a stable background for economic activity.[23]

The problem of controlling money, or more likely, failing to control it goes a long way towards explaining why we have inflation. "The Federal government is the engine of inflation—the only one there is."[24] Neither wage demands of unions nor administered prices of our monopolistic corporations nor, apparently, OPEC's pricing policies are to blame for inflation, at least not in the measure that the government is at fault. Washington, D.C. finances its spending increases and budget deficits with tax increases or, more likely, with the printing of money. The failure to align the money supply with real economic growth means that we are taxed by inflation rather than by statutory decree.[25] This practice is dishonest and, in the long run, untenable as a policy; we can assume that it touches, quite directly, upon urban America and upon all of the constituent elements of the economy.

A number of other approaches to the economy are consistent with monetarism. They are based on Friedman's hard evidence, set out in his Nobel lecture, that inflation and unemployment are usually found together in all modern capitalist economies. The evidence is contrary to the inverse relationship of the two, a basic assumption of Keynesian economics, and the reason for the development of the relationship's analytical device, the Phillips curve.[26] Another correlative approach, which is really a strategy more than anything else, is to plump for tax cuts even in the face of huge budget deficits. The logic is simple: budget-tinkering is a process that may become isolated from revenue-raising. If taxes are raised in order to meet the problem of budget deficits, the spenders in government will stretch revenues to cover as many new programs and increased outlays as possible. If, on the other hand, revenues are slashed, adjustments will be required. The deeper the cut, the bigger the adjustments. This is why Friedman could support the huge slash in property tax revenues promoted by Proposition 13 in California in 1978, and it accounts for his support of a constitutional amendment to peg federal revenues to the percentage of real economic growth occuring each year.[27] There is a great deal of the meat axe in this approach, to be sure, but Friedman is not bothered by it; he believes that many government programs are totally unnecessary.

Monetarism has been in vogue in recent years. Governments have been eager to try the Friedman formula. Chile and Israel, both on direct advice from Friedman, failed to achieve any gains in the fight against inflation, and Margaret Thatcher and her Conservative government in Britain have not, so far, had much more return than increases in both prices and the unemployment rate.[28] The Reagan administration seems both enthusiastic and chary. Friedman, of course, has an out. It can always be shown that certain circumstances, such as an economy's structural features or the failure to follow some minor guideline of monetarist policy, have proved fatal to the hope of any sure test. Friedman has shown a marvelous capacity for tracking down minutiae that prove his point; anyone familiar with his rewriting of economic history knows this.

The discipline of economics can always be relied upon, however, to produce dissent against almost anything proffered by one of their own. A range of economists, from liberal John Kenneth Galbraith to conservative former Federal Reserve Board Chairman Arthur Burns, is dubious about the ability of any government to define, much less control, the money supply.[29] Governor Henry Wallich of the Federal Reserve Board, for example, who has excellent credentials as an inflation-fighter and who is no leftist radical, says that changes in interest rates lead to changes in the economy. Changes in the growth rate of the money supply, on the other hand, seem coincident with changes in the economy. "Moreover," he adds, "it's easy to understand how interest rate changes can influence spending decisions by businessmen and consumers. The connection with money isn't that clear."[30] But Friedman, in the final analysis, does not hold out as much hope for money supply regulation as is generally believed:

> I believe that the potentiality of monetary policy in offsetting other forces making for instability is far more limited than is commonly believed. We simply do not know enough to be able to recognize minor disturbances when they occur or to be able to predict . . . what monetary policy is required to offset their effects. . . . Experience suggests that the path of wisdom is to use monetary policy explicitly to offset other disturbances only when they offer a "clear and present danger."[31]

This is a rather amazing admission for one whose whole career seems to be animated by a fervent desire for control of the money supply. The failure to establish this control has supposedly led to inflation, creating encroachments on the value of the dollar and hardships for those on fixed incomes, for savers, for consumers, and for small businesses forced to borrow at high interest rates. It also affects nearly all taxpayers, who suffer the pains of "bracket creep" when their inflation-level incomes rise, placing them in a higher tax category without a commensurate gain in their standard of living. Friedman has proposed a constitutional amendment that would require an indexing of income in accordance with the rate of inflation, intended to prevent "bracket creep."[32]

The problem of "bracket creep" is just one more example of government gone wrong and is no accident, according to Friedman.

Government, like the free enterprise system, has an "invisible hand" operating it, but this hand is represented by the machinations of politics. It therefore operates in a direction precisely the opposite of the invisible hand in the market.[33] Government, for example, will spend citizens' money with less care than the citizens themselves would. Government operates in terms of political brokerage, not market brokerage, and the result of its bargains are invariably at odds with the "economic sense" of the market. In addition, government fails to live up to its own terms of reference, holding itself out to be something better than what it is. In Friedman's opinion, "the growth of the bureaucracy, reinforced by the changing role of the courts, has made a mockery of . . . 'a government of laws instead of men'."[34]

The trouble is more than just the venality of government. It is in the nature of the system, which Friedman describes as pluralist. Many observers, the great economist points out, believe that our society and government are elite-ruled rather than pluralist. They see independent regulatory commissions taken over by the very industries they are meant to regulate. They see Congress and the bureaucracy bowing to the powerful. But appearances are deceptive. What is occurring most of the time is that special interests are seeking some rather narrowly defined benefit that will enrich them; meanwhile, the general public is not aroused by the issue simply because the marginal difference in the cost of government is so little in comparison with the great advantage being won by the special interests. Friedman believes that elite-rule theorists and believers look upon government as an arena in which special interests fight out a zero-sum game; that is, what is gained by one interest will be lost by another. The reality, he asserts, is that these special interests continually beat us, the general public, in a battle for what seems to them to be a nearly unlimited pie.[35] For this reason, Friedman proposes another constitutional amendment, one to limit taxing powers and therefore to limit spending. Tax increases would be geared to a proportion of the gross national product. The effect, he says, would be to turn the special interests upon one another rather than upon us.[36] The practical goal would be to reduce the number of special interest laws. Ideally, of course, all such laws should be abolished. Even the special interests, Friedman claims, would be better off.[37]

One might expect that Friedman, since he eschews elite-rule theory, would be immune to declarations about distant "others" who have appropriated power illegitimately. But Friedman is an American conservative, and is therefore wholly susceptible to this affliction, which is shared by Banfield, Buckley, Ayn Rand, and especially by Irving Kristol. Friedman goes to the length of specifically endorsing Kristol's idea of a "new class" of dissatisfied, antibusiness intellectuals sitting in places of importance in the media, universities, foundations, and bureaucracy. In many other contexts, Friedman alludes to intellectuals and bureaucrats in a pejorative fashion, and he sets out his belief that this new elite has initiated government projects and legislation in the name of "doing good" when in fact the general public is either opposed to, or indifferent to, such ideas.[38]

The tragedy is that these intellectuals are only fooling themselves, says Friedman. If present trends continue and we become a collectivist society, "the intellectuals who have done so much to drive us down the path will not be the ones who run the society; the prison, the insane asylum, or the graveyard will be their fate."[39] Friedman's conservative views, then, embrace an apocalyptic vision of the future, unless, of course, we become good conservatives and rein in the government. And who is to say he is wrong? History is a story of misery and oppression for most people. A broad spectrum of views—the New Left activists of the 1960s, for example—shares Friedman's worries about bureaucracy and intrusive government. He does manage, however, to keep the huge multinational corporations out of his nightmares. They are less of a worry because, after all, they are "private." (Friedman does admit, as one would expect, that "our markets are far from completely free.")[40] The essence of Professor Friedman's list of selected dangers, it seems, is that big government is not merely costly, or meddling, or inefficient, or wasteful, or purposeless. It is a threat to individual freedom: "We are going down a path which will destroy our free society. . . . If we continue the growth of government and its continuing involvement in our lives, it will destroy us. It has gone a long way toward destroying a free society now."[41] The free market and the free society are only compatible with a free system of government; big government is only compatible with tyranny. Indeed, it *is* tyranny. Friedman believes, with Ayn Rand, that the ruling principle of political systems is conformity. This conformity is extended under tyranny, but it even exists in a free system, since the minority losing on an issue or in an election must give in to the majority. Politics is therefore always at odds with individual freedom and with the free market, which is an expression of individual freedom.[42]

Economic and political life also have a symmetry about them, however, and this is the theme of the Friedmans' testament, *Free to Choose*. (Rose Friedman, the economist's wife, is co-author.) The Friedmans see their task as one of defining the relationship of the government and the economy so that those things which are difficult or impossible to achieve through voluntary exchange can be accomplished jointly with the government. In this view, both systems, political and economic, are regarded as markets in which the outcomes are determined by the interactions of persons pursuing their own self-interests rather than by the social goals the participants claim for their motivations.[43] It is a cynical view, to be sure, but it corresponds to the belief in the two kinds of "invisible hands"—one in the market, one in politics and government—and the interests that these hands pursue.

The thesis begins to break down when it is applied. There is an economic freedom, it is asserted, which corresponds to each of the political freedoms listed in the Bill of Rights. This is the symmetry. The prohibition of freedom of speech is absolutely forbidden by the First Amendment, for example, and there is "no consideration of each case on its merits." It becomes necessary, then, to establish an equivalent of the First Amendment in the economic arena, or an economic bill of rights, which would limit and restrict government entry and/or regulation. Such an amendment to the Constitution would not, by itself, guarantee anything. Other amendments are proposed to fulfill these purposes. But such an amendment would help to create the right climate of opinion.[44] One is compelled to ask whether any analogy should be made between free speech and the market concept of freedom. Many of the poor and even of the middle class see a part of their economic freedom ensured or enhanced by governmental activity.[45] It is wrong, in the first place, to put such an absolutist interpretation on the First Amendment. Justice Hugo Black notwithstanding, the courts do not support that interpretation; whether they should do so or not is another matter. There is, of course, an operative presumption in the law in favor of free speech, but this hardly assures victory on a consistent basis for the cause of free speech.

Friedman also proposes constitutional amendments to establish a flat rate rather than a graduated income tax, a "sound money" policy to limit the range of monetary growth, the tax-indexing amendment already mentioned, a limitation on federal taxes and the requirement of a balanced budget, a prohibition of tariffs, a prohibition on wage and price controls, and an end to all occupational licensing for doctors, attorneys, barbers, plumbers, and others. "This is hardly an exhaustive list," Friedman adds, because "we still have three to go to match the ten amendments in the original Bill of Rights."[46] How's that for symmetry? While the Friedmans are looking for three more amendments in order to set up a perfect match, they have also suggested that it might be possible to collapse some of the above items into more all-inclusive, omnibus-type amendments. The tariffs, wage and price controls, and occupational licensing amendments, for example, are said to be amenable to this kind of treatment. This amendment would read: "The right of the people to buy and sell legitimate goods and services at mutually acceptable terms shall not be infringed by Congress or any of the States." This amendment is held to be analogous to the Second Amendment, "which guarantees the right to keep and bear arms." This particular analogy rests upon a shaky ground since two Supreme Court decisions, one in 1876 and one in 1939, have definitively ruled that the Second Amendment offers no such guarantee.[47]

But none of the analogies hold in this whole absurd exercise. Friedman treats the Constitution as a toy to meddle with freely for the sake of his own idiosyncratic views of government and economics. Perhaps his apocalyptic belief about the path we are taking is the reason for his doing so, but that does not excuse a proposal as full of holes as this one is. As if this wholesale approach to Constitution-writing is not bad enough, Friedman also calls for a constitutional convention, which would be far more dangerous than any of his proposed amendments. This could result in the loss of the Bill of Rights freedoms we now enjoy.[48]

Friedman feels confident of the trends. In his 1980 book, *Free to Choose*, he says that people are finally "waking up" to the dangers of big government and collectivism and that the country may reverse its course.[49] People are perhaps beginning to recognize the advantages of laissez-faire capitalism. They may be beginning to understand that the market confers the advantages of contract and that government can only confer the advantages of status. This was the situation, of course, before the rise of modern capitalism. Friedman explains further that capitalism is progressive. It has freed people from the dictates of a system of status. Socialists and a lot of liberals are really reactionary rather than progressive; they seek to return us to the time when status, rather than contract, counted for something, and when, not incidentally, it was government, and not the market, that defined social and economic relationships.[50]

Friedman would go far, probably farther than most people, to remove the burdens of government. National parks should be operated by private enterprise.[51] The right to sell liquor, permits to operate gambling establishments, or licenses and franchises for taxis would be auctioned off by the government to the highest bidders.[52] The right to practice any trade or profession would not be subject to any licensing, nor would any standards or credentials be required by a professional association.[53] The draft is opposed, not so much on libertarian grounds but because it violates market pricing of military service. Friedman favors the legalization of marijuana, and perhaps of some other drugs, because the market pricing of these items and their availability would tend to undercut the illegal drug trade and cut the crime rate as well.[54]

The market is the invariable criterion in Friedman's conservatism. Why, he was asked, does General Motors waste capital expenditures by offering forty-seven Chevrolet models to the public? "There are forty-seven models because that is what consumers want."[55] Friedman would not be impressed if you told him that the geniuses of General Motors could have used capital more efficiently had they anticipated consumer demand for small cars; they might not have suffered a loss of half a billion dollars in 1980. It is the beauty of the free market that one can suffer losses as well as gains. Never mind that valuable resources are wasted on forty-seven models, or on stackable potato chips that are not really potato chips, or on picture telephones never developed beyond prototypes. Never mind that some of our garment factories are sweatshops that, Friedman admits, "violate many of the standards that we now regard as every worker's right." Most of the workers there are "immigrants from a distant country. A place like this gives them a chance to get started."[56] Unless, of course, the boss works them to death or some uninspected piece of machinery kills or maims them.

What is the market, anyway? Is it merely the right to exploit those who are economically weak, regardless of the law? Apparently so, given Friedman's steadfast prohibition of almost any and all regulations. A related question is, when is a profit merely a profit and when is it gouging? If an oil well makes a three-dollar profit on "old oil" at a regulated price of six dollars, is it fair to deregulate this price so that it can go up to the monopoly price (few argue that OPEC is a free-market force) of forty dollars a barrel, producing a profit of thirty-seven dollars? Friedman would answer affirmatively. In fact, "we cannot have a free market if Exxon is not permitted to make excess profits.[57] These Exxon excesses must continue, because the desire for profits stimulates the corporation to provide for energy reserves.[58]

The market, in short, is what the pricing system makes it. And that applies to anything. When asked whether a chemist ought to accommodate the economic system and a particular business firm by making napalm, Friedman had a matter-of-fact answer that embraced the market system and the pricing mechanism that regulates it:

> If a chemist feels it is immoral to make napalm, he can solve his problem by getting a job where he doesn't have to. He will pay a price. But the ultimate effect will be that if many, many people feel that way, the cost of hiring people to make napalm will be high, napalm will be expensive, and less of it will be used.[59]

Napalm may be immoral, but the market is amoral. It treats napalm like it treats any other commodity, with adjustments made for those who do not want to be connected with it.

Secondary sources on Milton Friedman tend to paint his philosophy as that of libertarian rightist, and he may himself prefer such a description of his market approach to virtually all political questions. All the same, the approach to the morality of using napalm could be said to contrast markedly with what many people would call libertarian or even humane, so it is possible that such descriptions of his views are too generous.

The amorality of the market carries over into an amoral political system in other ways. Friedman chooses, for example, to let business people off the hook on the question of making bribery payments to public officials abroad in order to win contracts or receive favored treatment. He points out that the issue is not the venality of business; it is instead the venality of governments, since their officials are the recipients of the bribes and therefore are to blame for this unwholesome set of circumstances.[60] Is it acceptable, then, to consider that receiving a bribe is bad but paying one or offering one is all right?

There is quite a remarkable paradox in Friedman's insistence, on the one hand, that government intervention in the economy is profoundly immoral—a term he applies, for example, to wage and price controls—while, on the other hand, he adopts what could charitably be described as a clinical or technician's view of his work as an economic adviser. Some would call this activity amoral. Working for the brutal and repressive government of Chile in 1976, Friedman says, was a matter of rendering "technical economic advice," which he does not consider an "evil."[61] This is no different, he claims, than the technical advice a physician would offer to the Chilean government, or any government, to help end a plague.[62]

Others would disagree; the late Orlando Letelier, who had first-hand knowledge of Chile's authoritarian ways, wrote:

> It is curious that a man who wrote a book, *Capitalism and Freedom,* to . . . (argue) that only classical economic liberalism (market capitalism) can support political democracy,

can now so easily disentangle economics from politics when the economic theories he advocates coincide with an absolute restriction of every type of democratic freedom. One would logically expect that . . . those who impose 'unrestrained economic freedom' would also be held responsible when . . . this policy is inevitably accompanied by massive repression, hunger, unemployment, and the permanence of a brutal police state.[63]

Friedman is also on record, after all, with statements such as: "There is no such thing as a purely economic issue," and there is an "intimate connection between political freedom and economic freedom."[64]

Friedman later felt compelled to denounce the totalitarianism of Chile.[65] It is most commendable that he did recognize these realities at some point. It cannot be said, however, that this episode demonstrates prescience or foresight, or even understanding, in matters of political economy.

The Chilean affair illustrates several considerations important to ponder. It shows that Friedman can easily, much too easily, slip back and forth between an insistence on certain moral imperatives and other perspectives that must be termed amoral. It reveals, of course, that he can also be mistaken, a good fact to keep in mind since some people tend to be overawed by Nobel prize-winners. It clearly indicates, most of all, that the so-called free market is compatible, ironic as it may seem, with repressive, dictatorial government. By definition a market cannot be truly free under such circumstances, but, all too often, it can give a political system a character that seems quite satisfactory to Milton Friedman and many "free market" conservatives. Nothing is perfect, after all, and so rationalizations can be artlessly developed.

Weaknesses of perception and what amounts to a double standard of judgment wrought by ideological blinders are obvious in some other common features of Friedman's work. His rewriting of economic and political history to prove the beneficence of capitalism tends to downplay the brutal aspects of American industrial development and the loathsome and dishonest activities of the robber barons.[66] Facile comparisons of the economies of various countries can be very galling as Friedman ignores some of the most elementary cultural, historical, and even economic considerations, such as the presence or availability of natural resources.[67] This failing can be most misleading to the layman who may read a Friedman column in *Newsweek* or some other popular periodical. Friedman's policy prescriptions also display the double standard: antitrust laws are not such a good tool against corporate monopoly, he tells us, for there are other ways to achieve the same ends; at the same time, the laws are well worth applying to labor unions.[68]

There is a consistent fealty to "the market," but is libertarianism always obvious or even, at times, terribly important to Friedman? It appears that it is not.

There is terrific symbolism and irony in Friedman's choice of an opening quotation for his book, *Free to Choose*. In it, the dissenting opinion of Justice Louis Brandeis admonishes us to be "most on our guard when the government's purposes are beneficial," and we are told about the dangers to liberty that emanate from "men of zeal, well-meaning but without understanding."[69] The decision with which Brandeis disagreed is *Olmstead v. U.S.* (1928), a case in which the Supreme Court upheld wiretapping practices as long as none of the wiretapping equipment or devices were protruding through the inner wall of a house. The doctrine of trespass was used by the Court to define this issue of personal civil liberties.[70] Trespass, as everyone knows, is a property rights concept, and property rights are Friedman's fundamental prop of market capitalism. *Olmstead* was later overturned by the Court, which realized the absurd inappropriateness of applying a property rights concept to an even more fundamental human right. Brandeis recognized this in the very dissent which Friedman picked to begin his best-selling book about market capitalism—a dissent actually criticizing the overimportance of property and market capitalism. And the irony does not end there, for Brandeis could have been describing Friedman (who wears neckties with Adam Smith medallions on them whenever he can) when the justice warned of "men of zeal, well-meaning but without understanding."[71]

Friedman's Urban Vision

Devotion to the late twentieth-century version of Adam Smith's free market and to the policies of monetarism is an outlook that can have far-reaching effects upon urban life. This devotion, nevertheless, can affect more than just our cities. It can establish a framework for fiscal policy, our defense posture, and other considerations not necessarily urban in their impact. How does Friedman look at the city, its problems and challenges, and its place in American life?

Obviously he is very pro-city in his own way. Friedman believes in localism, and his writings show that he is nearly always referring to cities when he talks about local government. The Founding Fathers saw the benefits of local and decentralized government; that is good enough for Friedman, and he prefers state government to federal government; local government, including the cities, is better than the state. "The more distant the source of power," says the economist, "the more difficult it is to have truly representative and responsible government."[72] Unfortunately, we have seen a tremendous growth in government at all levels and a great transfer of power from local government and local control to centralized government and control, all accomplished in the name of security and equality.[73] A great mishmash of direct grants, grants-in-aid, and various other arrangements has distorted the meaning of local government and has accomplished virtually nothing. It is claimed, says Friedman, that federal programs will assist the less-endowed states and areas of the nation. What actually occurs, he insists, is that money is taken from all fifty states and returned to all fifty, "roughly in proportion to the amounts contributed."[74] In this assertion, the figures show that Friedman is just plain wrong. The usual rank-ordering of the states in terms of federal dollars received shows that while some receive much more than they provide in revenues others receive as little as 70 percent of their revenues. *Consumers Research* magazine, for example, indicates that Michigan receives only 76¢ for every dollar while Mississippi takes in $1.65 and Alaska receives $1.82.[75]

Localism is also supported by Friedman because he thinks it means lower taxes. The more local control of government spending and programs, the less spending there will be.[76] The ultimate answers to the spending question, of course, lie in the Friedman constitutional amendment tying taxation to a steady percentage of the gross national product and the amendment requiring a balanced federal budget.

Urbanization is often used as an excuse for the development of massive federal programs and spending. A limited government, leave-it-alone policy was feasible, acording to this argument, in a sparsely settled nineteenth-century America. But this is specious, says Friedman. "One hour in Hong Kong will dispose of that view."[77] Hong Kong is one of Friedman's more famous adventures into superficial comparisons. The Crown Colony is considered to have a relatively uncontrolled and laissez-faire type of economy, giving the lie to the need for regulations, labor unions, or the welfare state; but it is not politically free. Its citizens have virtually no voice in government.[78]

Federalism and, quite often, local government gives us uniform standards in education, sanitation, housing, building codes, and many public services. Some of these standards raise the level of these services and programs and perhaps even improve the lives of the people affected by them. Nevertheless, uniformity, Friedman believes, must be seen for what it is—basically antilocal in nature. And in any event, government, whether federal, state, or local, cannot match the diversity and variety of people and their individual actions. Therefore government should be discouraged from establishing any uniformities at any level.[79]

The uniformities sought by Friedman are quite another matter. They include his many proposed amendments to the U.S. Constitution, some of which—the antilicensing measure, for example—would directly affect the powers of local governments. They also include his approach to government at all levels, whether local or national: do as little as possible, and do that as cheaply as possible. (Perhaps—we are not sure—the national defense budget is excluded from this mandate for economy.) The approach is commendable from the standpoint of economy in government and in the view of many people of different political persuasions who view centralized decision making with suspicion. However, the various levels of government are diverse in their separate missions, programs, services, and purposes, and this diversity dictates some measure of pragmatism rather than a comprehensive penury and near-anarchism.

Friedman's blanket approach to the purposes of government at any level includes a maxim for local government: all possible functions should be performed by private companies or agencies. This applies to garbage collection, fire protection, or any service we normally expect from cities. Friedman is ideological to the maximum degree on this point. Private enterprise is cheaper, more efficient, and will invariably perform a better service; numerous studies will back him using the businesslike measure of cost-effectiveness, and that is all there is to that.[80]

Friedman also prefers localism because at the lowest levels of government, the city and the community level, the most innovation and incentive will be in evidence. He cites with approval the "sweat equity" people of the South Bronx who are seeking to improve apartment houses in order to make them serve again as homes.[81]

But these people, like so many others, receive federal assistance to help them with their projects, and many of us have grown to expect this kind of assistance. This, after all, is how the modern welfare state operates, particularly in an urban environment. The welfare state, encompassing not just welfare payments, but housing assistance, redevelopment loans, minimum wage laws, Social Security, government-paid health care, and poverty programs, among others, undergirds our cities' economies, governments, and people.

Nonetheless, the welfare state runs counter to the ideal of a free market economy or a laissez-faire state. It therefore forms no part of Friedman's urban vision. Even on its own terms, Friedman declares the welfare state a failure. The poor are not helped particularly. Most antipoverty programs and programs in education, in housing and urban renewal, and most certainly Social Security, involve a transfer of income from groups who are less well off to those who are in middle- or higher-income ranges. The only exception is Aid for Families with Dependent Children, the welfare program most often referred to as "welfare," and this accounts for its unpopularity.[82] How can the poor be helped by rent subsidies paid to middle-income families? How are they helped by the disruptions and displacement caused by urban renewal that destroys more homes than it builds? Friedman attacks even the sacred cow of higher education subsidies, calling them the methods by which Beverly Hills parents send their offspring to college at the expense of the people in the ghetto of Watts.[83]

Nor are the responses of the poor to welfare state programs necessarily those envisioned by their original authors. Friedman points out that the poor often resent the regimentation of their lives by social workers and other bureaucrats. The poor tend to reject public housing if it is possible for them to do so.[84] They pick up stakes, disrupting family and community life in order to move to other places—New York City is a good example—that are more generous in their welfare programs and payments.[85] In one sense at least, this latter activity should be applauded by Friedman, for it corresponds to the workings of the "invisible hand" of the Adam Smith free market.

Friedman's descriptions show that the welfare state corrupts the moral fabric, weakens family ties, and encourages demands for more welfare and more poverty programs even as poverty and social needs decline. Like Banfield and Kristol, Adam Smith's disciple states that the poverty line tends to rise continuously in line with our success in eradicating poverty. No one, after all, is ever satisfied with the prevailing distribution of income.[86]

We have been led to believe that there is a basic human right to live at some minimal level (which, it should be noted, is the raison d'etre of the welfare state), that we have a basic human right to "food, shelter, and medical care without a quid pro quo."[87] But these rights are simply not possible because, well, for one thing, welfare programs have created obstacles to making them possible, and secondly, because such matters can best be handled by voluntary action. There can be no "right" to economic security. The closest we can come to insuring people against misfortune is to encourage private charity. Indeed, the greatest damage to the spirit and impulse of charity has been wrought by the welfare state. It is time to return to private charity, to try to match the good old days of the nineteenth century when charity was in its heyday.[88]

Well and good. After all, who can possibly be opposed to charity? The answer is conservatives. Not Friedman, obviously, but Ayn Rand, who probably has as many followers in the conservative movement as Friedman does, and who condemns private acts of charity as well as the welfare state. (About all that can be said is that she does not favor punishing those who are charitable.) And there is evidence that conservatives take her lesson to heart. For instance, the tax returns of Ronald Reagan, released during the 1980 campaign, show that he contributes far less than one percent of his income to charity.

The alternative to charity, according to Friedman, is grim to behold. It is the welfare state running amok, a situation exemplified by such dreary economies as those of Great Britain, Sweden, and, in our own country, New York City.[89] New York is the perfect example of the results of an over-generous and ill-administered welfare state. The only difference between it and the national welfare states is that New York City cannot print money. It actually did the equivalent of this by selling dubious "moral obligation" bonds. The City probably spent enough to eradicate poverty many times over, but the waste, maladministration, and encouragement of in-migration have brought it to near-bankruptcy and now, Milton Friedman decrees, it is too late. The welfare state has so corroded political life in New York that a goodly part of the electorate is organized for, and committed to, the politics of the handout.[90]

Charity may not be sufficient to take care of the needs of the people of our cities, however. Friedman recognizes this, and he has worked out a negative income tax proposal, a system of automatic payments to the very poor coupled with incentives to get them off the dole. This proposal will be examined later. Meanwhile, since Friedman says that government has no responsibility in any kind of welfare endeavor, what institutions will support the urban community in combatting some of its very serious problems?[91]

A natural place to turn, as all cities do, is to the corporations that operate urban-based factories, stores, research and training centers, and headquarters offices. A doctrine of corporate social responsibility has surfaced in recent years, both a reaction to

Naderite crusades and a public relations consciousness. This doctrine is irrational, subversive and socialist, charges Friedman. Corporations have no responsibilities other than profit-maximization. He recognizes that on occasion a corporation can create some good will by sponsoring some local effort or activity but points out that even this should be carefully monitored, for a corporation essentially has no money. Any activities carried out in the name of social responsibility are costs passed on to customers, stockholders, or employees.[92] This is why corporate taxes make no sense at all. Taxes are merely another cost passed on in higher prices. Instead of levying a corporation tax, the government should tax each shareholder on the appropriate number of shares according to the earnings-per-share figures. Talk about disincentives for investment! At the same time, Friedman opposes the tax deduction made available for charitable corporate contributions.[93]

The public is full of misperceptions on the issue of corporate social responsibility, says Friedman, and he offers some rather graphic examples. This additional cost to corporations is at odds with the purposes of the corporation. No one asserts, he says, that the corner "Mom and Pop" grocery store should sell its merchandise below cost in order to help its poor customers. It would soon be out of business. The same principle applies to a big business. Most assume, says Friedman, that companies would only help "good guy" causes. Why assume this? The big corporations of early-1930s Germany gave money to Hitler and the Nazis. One must agree that Friedman makes a solid point here. He argues further that there is a great tendency to associate corporations with the wealthy people who founded them or run them. Henry Ford is an example: certainly he created great wealth for himself, but he and his company also created great wealth and provided a good product for the people.[94]

This strange set of assertions creates a view of corporations that probably very few city mayors or officials, to cite just one group, would consider realistic. Friedman believes that corporations have no responsibility to society, in fact, no responsibility other than profit making. At the same time, they really have no money. No responsibility and no money? How then do they amass great political power, which few deny that they have? Indeed, corporations

hold a central place in the elite structures of political power in
every one of America's cities, a fact confirmed by every
community power study from Middletown to Regional City. Their
decisions in such areas as labor relations, expansion of plant and
equipment, location, and finance have profound economic, political,
and social effects. And corporate political action committees and
their slush funds have become the scandal of our electoral
system.

There is another confusion here, one that is compounded by a
recent Supreme Court decision and perhaps some trends in the
law. Anglo-Saxon traditions in the law have always coupled
"rights" with "responsibilities" or "duties." Throughout their
history, American corporations have not been accorded Bill of
Rights freedoms, such as freedom of speech, because they have
not been regarded, despite the common fiction, as entities that
could claim such rights. In a rather revolutionary way, we now
seem to be moving away from these traditions, and corporations
are being accorded "rights." And if they are, they should surely
be assigned the corollary of "responsibilities," Friedman notwithstanding. Among such responsibilities, one could surely expect
to find the payment of taxes.

A central concern in assessing any thinker's urban vision is
his/her views on race relations, for this will undoubtedly continue
to be the make-or-break set of issues in the future of the cities.
For Friedman, the starting point is, as always, the market. The
capitalistic free market system is the best hope for urban blacks and
other minorities for several reasons: 1) Experience shows that "great
progress" has been made by blacks and others because of the
market system.[95] 2) "The market is a system of proportional
representation" that "protects the interests of minorities." Blacks,
Jews, and even the radically leftist Students for a Democratic
Society (SDS) should therefore support free enterprise capitalism.[96]
3) The growth of the free market system and the prosperity assured
by this growth tends to reduce the distrust and enmity of the
majority and therefore works against scapegoating. Unfortunately,
Friedman believes, minority groups have probably been less
enthusiastic, historically, about the free market than they should
be. In his view, minorities do not seem to realize how much they
need capitalism.[97]

According to Friedman, the bureaucrats and anti-free market forces in our society, by contrast, have set up policies and programs that have hurt blacks and other minorities. The welfare system has produced a paternalism that impairs the freedom and dignity of the recipients while weakening the structure of families. Unemployment is rife among black teenagers, and they have minimum-wage legislation to thank for it. Public housing has reinforced ghetto patterns of living as well as the despair and juvenile delinquency that go with them. Urban renewal has destroyed homes and disrupted lives. The public schools have also let down blacks and may actually have held them down.[98] Friedman's list of grievances goes on; and it must be admitted, despite specific disagreements that one could reasonably have with Friedman in evaluating these policies, the total result of all of this liberal legislation and administration has been far from encouraging.

The conservatism of Milton Friedman's market city, which is his urban vision, can hardly be cheering, either. His assertion that blacks have made "great progress" because of capitalism, for example, is not very convincing when it is remembered that government—and let us give it its due when it is deserved—abolished discrimination in its hiring practices long before discrimination was reduced on any significant scale in the private sector. In addition, it is difficult to understand what Friedman means by the "proportional representation" of the market when he never explains it. He may be correct in saying that the growth of prosperity for all helps to allay and quiet our distrust and scapegoating; but if American urban society is now going to participate in a zero-sum game, as some economists say, rather than in more or less continuous economic growth, which can hardly be guaranteed by monetarist or other policies, scapegoating and fear-mongering may flourish, working hand in hand with the capitalist system in ways that Friedman does not foresee.

In the meantime Friedman remains confident that there is, and shall continue to be, a strong correlation between capitalism and tolerance towards minorities. A free market does not take on irrelevant characteristics of inefficiency, he says. "The purchaser of bread does not know whether it was made from wheat grown by a white man or a Negro or a Christian or a Jew." In fact, there is an economic cost in discrimination which must be paid by the discriminator. The range of choice of bigots is more limited than it is with those who are free to choose. Refusal to hire or work alongside a minority group member requires a higher price to be paid or a lower return for work performed. Unfortunately, the record shows that many people and businesses, including some of our largest corporations, have been willing to pay such a price in the past and may well be continuing to do so. Friedman decries unfair treatment based merely upon the dislike of someone's race, skin color, sex, or religion. But he falls into a terrible error when he says, "It is hard to see that discrimination can have any meaning other than a 'taste' of others that one does not share." Such tastes cannot be coerced, so it is foolish to demand or enforce fair employment practices legislation.[99]

This is not an objection by Friedman to affirmative action laws, an objection made by many libertarian antiracists. Rather, this is a denunciation of *any* government attempt to instill or enforce attitudes regarding fair employment practices even though our national experience indicates that this, at a minimum, is necessary and even though fair employment enforcement may help produce a job market free of the distortions created by discrimination. What alternative does he propose? The answer, as always, is the same: rely upon the free market. The incredible naiveté about the free market even extends to an "invisible hand" that will wipe out discrimination. The competition for workers among employers and the competition among workers for jobs is expected, quite magically, to take care of the problem on the grounds that American cities and their suburbs have such a large variety of employers.[100] This is not the kind of world to which minorities, certainly unemployed minorities, can relate. The invisible hand is, in this instance, truly invisible.

Friedman's complete failure to understand race relations is obvious in his endorsement of a school voucher system in Virginia, a segregationist plot there to thwart equal opportunity in education. Again we have an example of ideological considerations carrying Friedman along; he supports school voucher systems even when their pernicious purpose is to undermine the law and, with it, the rights of blacks. Friedman claims that he prefers integration to segregation, but this preference is certainly not a very strong one.[101]

Like all the other conservative thinkers in this study, Friedman strikes out on race relations basically because he is not interested in the principle of equality. In fact, he is an adamant foe of equality. Friedman would demur on this charge by saying that neither equality before God nor equality of opportunity present problems for liberty, but that insistence upon equality of outcome or result does.[102] He feels that enforcement of equality, whether in housing, schools, or jobs, promotes discontent, resentment, and even violence.[103] Which raises the question: is this *really* a reason for not enforcing the law? Many conservatives would have trouble accepting such a proposition. The promotion of equality is also said to foster economic controls that not only restrict the free market, but also adversely affect the freedom of speech, press, and religion. Those receiving beneficence of the state would hesitate, for example, to criticize bureaucrats, policies, politicians, or programs for fear of economic sanctions. No one can gainsay that point. There is also a breakdown of law, because interference "with people's pursuit of their own values" will make them "try to find a way around."[104]

Friedman is not as strident as Irving Kristol or Ayn Rand in asserting that an urban "new class" of media people, educators, intellectuals, and bureaucrats has been behind the drive for equality. But he believes this, all the same, and he offers this new class and all egalitarians some advice: "You can . . . estimate what money income would correspond to your concept of equality. If your actual income is higher than that, you can keep that amount and distribute the rest to people who are below that level."[105] For himself and the other enthusiasts for the City of the Right, Friedman prefers the vision of the free market. As an ombudsman for the poor, the blacks, or for any citizen who is concerned about urban problems and services, Friedman would never succeed because he refers everyone to the same unhelpful department. But that is his urban vision. And, tragically, a vision is all it is.

Friedman's Urban Policies: Taxes, Income Security, Vouchers, and Laissez-Faire

Some of Friedman's policy suggestions and opinions have already been identified; his opposition to fair employment practices laws, to all professional licensing and credentialing, and to the regulation of drugs are examples. His seven sweeping constitutional amendment proposals, essentially aimed at controlling taxes, spending, and government regulation, are also based upon the momentums and motivations of opposition to the liberal welfare state.

It is only fair, however, to point out that Friedman is not simply and inevitably against things. Much more than any of the other four thinkers who are subjects of this study, he is willing to develop and present alternative policies for consideration. Sometimes this is done grudgingly; the alternative is proposed because Friedman believes that it is politically impossible to do away entirely with some of the guarantees of the welfare state. Ideally, laissez-faire should reign, but this is not an ideal world. On other occasions an alternative is proposed because it is believed that it will result in cost savings, efficiency, or less governmental control of our lives. Whatever the reason, Friedman must be given credit for being something more than one of those many conservatives who sit around saying nay to everything. More than this, he must be acknowledged as an innovative and creative source of policy proposals.

Taxation is an issue area of special concern to Milton Friedman, probably because he is an economist and because he feels that one of our greatest problems is excessive spending at all levels of government. He helped lead the fight against the local property tax in California in 1978, and he strongly believes that expenditures on urban programs do not help the poor.[106] Much of the money is used "to buy land or buildings or services from the not-so-poor . . . [or] to provide amenities for the not-so-poor." A great deal of the rest goes to pay handsome salaries to bureaucrats; and even the small amount which does trickle down to the poor is "largely wasted because it encourages them to substitute a handout for a wage." Thus the more money that is spent on the cities, the worse things become.[107]

Those who see some value in welfare state measures or poverty-related programs will of course regard Friedman's position as unhelpful. And none of his other positions on tax questions will be considered helpful either: end all corporation taxes, abandon all attempts to collect inheritance taxes, and change the graduated income tax to a flat rate tax in which everyone pays the same percentage of income without reference to the ability to pay. With respect to the latter, Friedman shows good evidence, as do many studies and sources, that the loopholes built into the income tax makes its supposedly graduated structure ineffective in helping the poor, anyway. It is the middle class that provides most government revenues. In exchange for the establishment of a flat rate, Friedman would favor doing away with all loopholes except for very strictly-accounted business expenses.[108] It might also be possible to reform the income tax by closing the loopholes and retaining the graduated system of payments, but Friedman will have none of this, despite the demonstrably beneficial effect it could have on the urban poor. One solution might be his demand to index income tax brackets for inflation. This would keep people from being pushed into ever-higher income brackets merely because their incomes look bigger as a result of inflation; and it is so important to Friedman that it is one of his proposed constitutional amendments.[109]

Since the tax system is such a central matter to Friedman, it is tied to his foremost welfare reform proposal, the negative income tax. This proposal has taken various forms over the years, but what it amounts to is a government support system for families whose incomes fall below a certain level. These families would receive payments from the government instead of paying taxes, and these payments would be automatic, would require no "means test" or other expensive accoutrements of welfare administration, and would decrease as the family moved up from poverty levels of income. Perhaps the most important feature of the system, as far as Friedman is concerned, is that incentives would be built into it to encourage individuals to become gainfully employed. The payments structure would taper off at just those precise times and levels that would best induce the recipients to find work. In addition, there would be no penalties attached to working and receiving part of one's income in that way. This is contrary to the present welfare system, which takes away a like amount of dollars of those earned.[110]

The negative income tax is seen as a replacement for the Aid to Families of Dependent Children program, and it is touted by Friedman as less expensive, in the long run, because it would do away with the great overhead costs of welfare administration, plus the reports, means tests, cumbersome application and checking procedures, and social workers prying into individuals' lives. The new system would give cash directly to the poor, the kind of aid most helpful to them. This cash benefit would do much to mitigate any need for such programs as the Comprehensive Employment and Training Act (CETA) public service jobs, food stamps, public housing, and many of the poverty remedies now wielded by the bureaucracy, including Social Security. The negative income tax would also promote self-esteem of the poor, give them incentives to do things for themselves, and withdraw many of the political factors now present in poverty programs and welfare administration.[111]

The implications of the negative income tax are very broad. Welfare administration would be taken out of the hands of Health and Human Services and placed under the Internal Revenue Service.[112] Income level would define explicitly where an individual would fit onto a list of chartered cash benefits. Most importantly, according to Friedman, the negative income tax would meet the specific needs which all welfare programs must fulfill from a political standpoint—reasonable cost, strong incentives to work, and a decent level of support for the recipient.[113] The plan's major difficulty, as with the present welfare system, is the reluctance of the American public, imbued with the virtues of the work ethic, to accept the idea of paying taxes, no matter how low, to guarantee a certain income level for others. This proved to be a problem when the Nixon administration considered a version of the negative income tax called the Family Assistance Plan. A further problem is the trade-off welfare recipients are expected to make. If the negative income tax guarantees are substantially lower than the levels of welfare received, the trade would be a poor one indeed. This, again, was one of the defects of the Family Assistance Plan. What perhaps finally killed FAP was that President Nixon arrived at a point in which he no

longer relished the idea of becoming a twentieth-century Disraeli—
that is, a conservative with social welfare pretensions.[114]

The negative income tax is nonetheless an extremely important
proposal to ponder for anyone who seeks to understand Friedman's
political stance, as well as the implications of his policies for the
cities. He does not, of course, support or endorse just *any* negative
income tax idea, but he appears open to some suggestions for
alterations in his proposal.[115] And if the funding levels for it are
sufficient, it appears to be, in the long run, a likely replacement
for the welfare system.

Another proposal central to understanding the character of
Friedman's urban policies is his insistence upon educational
voucher systems. Friedman has spilled more ink on this issue
than on any other political question, so it is obvious that he has
developed strong feelings as well as an adamant position.

Our educational history has been, from Friedman's viewpoint,
most unfortunate. Governmental control of education is a tradition
that is one of "an island of socialism in a free market sea." The
ability of Horace Mann and the educational establishment of
his day to bring about state control of this important function
rests essentially upon a distrust of the market. Today it is
largely the "new class" of leftish-inclined intellectuals who
promote and protect the public school system in an age in which it
is less defensible than ever before.[116] The "administration of
educational institutions by the government, the 'nationalization,'
as it were, of the bulk of the 'education industry' is . . . difficult to
justify on . . . any . . . grounds."[117] This fact of government control
is Friedman's "key" to understanding the problems of our
urban schools.[118]

The way out is to set up a system of payments to parents, to
be furnished in the form of vouchers, in order to enable them
to pick and choose among schools, private or public, in order to
find the most satisfactory educational environment for their
children. The vouchers would not cover all of the costs of
education, but would take care of a very substantial percentage
of these costs. Tax support for schools would become minimal or,
under ideal circumstances, would disappear altogether. Under this

"freedom to choose" system, a market type of competition would be bound to develop and, as is always the case with the market, the good would flourish and the bad would fall by the wayside. The result would be a much improved quality of education, as students—and parents' approval—are sought by schools and teachers.[119]

Beyond the enhancement of the freedom to choose and the improvement of educational quality, Friedman sees the voucher system as resulting in educational cost efficiencies, an amelioration of issues of economic class and of racial tensions, a possible end to conflict over the church-state issue in education, and an end to the need for a large, wasteful educational bureaucracy in our school districts and in Washington, D.C.[120] In addition, we should expect in time to see the development of many good, medium-priced, private schools.[121]

Blacks, he claims, would be helped considerably by educational vouchers because black parents could choose a school without considering such factors as its location. At the present time, public schools exacerbate racial tensions because the good ones are located in the wealthier and suburban neighborhoods while the worst ones are in the inner city.[122]

But private schools cause racial tensions as well, and Friedman and most conservatives have traditionally opposed integration of the public schools or have been indifferent to this question. Friedman, for example, is not only antibusing but also strongly opposes the centralized, state collection of educational funds and their distribution on a per-pupil basis to school districts in order to help poor districts and provide equal educational opportunity.[123] Much of the mess in education, then, can be assessed against conservatives as much, or perhaps more, than against the so-called public education establishment. Friedman's short-sightedness is perhaps most obvious when he discusses the equalization of educational funding: "But why stop with schooling? If it is wrong for different children to have different amounts spent on their schooling, how can it be right to have different amounts spent on their food? Housing? Clothing? Etc?"[124] Such an impulse breeds conformity, according to Friedman, a "homogenized" society that kills incentive. All of us want our children to attend a little bit better school, if that is possible; those who demand equality do not understand this.[125] Friedman believes that it may be necessary, even with a voucher system, to continue public financing of education for hardship cases. But compulsory attendance laws would no longer be needed.[126]

Is the market model à la Adam Smith really workable as a basis for our urban school systems or for any other school systems? The voucher system, according to various critics, could result in an increase in de facto racial segregation. It could endanger the constitutional separation of church and state rather than resolving church-state issues. Surely it would widen the gap of expenditures on rich children and poor children since much of the tax base for education would be removed. Public schools would stand in danger of becoming educational centers of last resort, prisonlike catchments for the unwanted. And it is possible that experts in the field, rather than parents, really know more about education and what to expect from it.[127] Christopher Jencks, who is politically on the Left and who advocates a regulated type of voucher plan, condemns the unregulated type advocated by Friedman, Buckley, Kristol, and other conservatives, saying "an unregulated voucher system would be the most serious setback for the education of disadvantaged children in the history of the United States."[128] All of Friedman's work and thought on this proposal, according to this view, does not save it from remaining a bad idea.

Higher education should likewise be financed by voucher systems, but should have its financing system combined with an extensive student loan program. This would induce competition in the same way as voucher systems at other levels would do; and all government subsidies of higher education should end.[129] In addition, Friedman would get rid of the "chilling effects" of government influence on higher education by doing away with research grants and subsidies from agencies like the National Science Foundation or the National Endowment for the Humanities, since these apparently represent a serious civil liberties problem.[130] Friedman ignores such blatant compromises of the academic spirit as the "chairs of free enterprise" and "chairs of private enterprise" proliferating around the country, however, and he also has no problem with any "chilling effects" of police being called into a campus. He feels that the latter move has sometimes become necessary in this age.[131]

The central point in favor of voucher systems, no matter what level of education is involved, is that they provide for competition and a kind of consumers' choice. Unfortunately, Friedman has little respect for the rights of consumers in other sectors of the economy:

> The basic premise of the consumer "crusade" is that unless the government moves in with inspectors and agencies, consumers will be defrauded by unethical producers and sellers. I can't accept that kind of solution. If a consumer finds he is being sold rotten meat at the grocery store, he has the very best protection agency available: the market. He simply stops trading at that store. . . . Eventually, the . . . seller gets the message and offers good meat or he goes out of business.[132]

It is all too simple. Abuse the public and you will go out of business. But in urban America, where businesses come and go and people come and go all the time, some assurances must be given to people that they will be treated fairly. It is all very well to say that consumer regulations, in either federal or municipal laws, do not prevent accidents or mistakes and use tris, the carcinogen found in childrens' night clothes, as an example. The fact is that consumer regulation saved America from the damage of the drug thalidomide. Looking at consumers' rights in a somewhat broader sense, it would have been a good thing, apparently, to have had stricter fire regulations in the Las Vegas Municipal Code in 1980, so that hotel guests' lives might have been saved. Friedman, who waxes hyperbolically on this issue, believes that the consumer movement and consumer laws are bad for consumers, since they cause products to be more expensive than they should be. Anyway, consumers have more than just the market to rely upon, he says, citing the protections offered by brand names, private testing organizations, and the hope of an eventual end to all trade barriers.[133]

Labor issues are another paramount concern. Like the other four subjects of this study, Friedman is an enthusiastic union-buster. More than any of the architects of the City of the Right, however, he tells why he finds unions so distasteful: They are corrupt and violent; they are a throwback to feudal guilds; they do not help the poor; they create unemployment; and they pressure government to provide such ridiculous laws and regulations as the minimum wage or the rules of the Occupational Safety and Health Administration. In many cities, and especially in New York, the municipal unions have proved to be a drain on the taxpayers and have brought governments to the brink of bankruptcy.[134] It should be hastily and prudently pointed out that they have also helped New York City stave off bankruptcy with pension-fund loans. And we know that corporate managments can also be corrupt, violent (especially against unions), capable of pressuring government, and even medieval in some of their habits and ways.

The real problems with unions are that they are monopolies protected and even fostered by government and that they achieve higher wages and benefits not from their employers, but at the expense of consumers. How, then, should cities deal with unions? What remedies are available? In Friedman's opinion, all government support and protection of unions should be abolished. No collective bargaining elections, no unfair labor practices charges or litigation, no National Labor Relations Board, nothing. At the same time, antitrust laws should be applied to unions in order to break them up.[135]

And what are workers to do under these circumstances? Friedman points out that they can take solace from the fact that our urban society provides them with many employers. Competition among these employers, even for poor, unskilled people, will be great enough to provide decent wages for employees. In the long run, such a benevolent system can be expected to work so well that the employees will achieve "real" wage gains out of technological and productivity improvements. The "invisible hand" again works its magic. Meanwhile, he urges that everything possible should be done to discourage labor unions. State "right-to-work" laws, which ban union shop contracts, should be enacted.[136] And minimum wage laws, about which Friedman has written a great deal, should be repealed or at least reduced to lower minimums.[137] Minimum-wage laws are created only because of labor unions' worry about competition from the low-wage areas of the Sun Belt, and Friedman feels that it serves the unions right that companies are moving to the Sun Belt and abandoning the Northeast and Midwest! Minimum wages are also the most "anti-Negro" laws ever enacted because they have caused unemployment among ghetto teenagers.[138]

Friedman disapproves of all public housing, all Federal Housing Administration (FHA) and VA mortgage programs, all urban renewal and redevelopment schemes, all housing subsidies, any rent control ordinances, and, for that matter, probably all HUD programs.[139] He favors indexing mortgage rates so that they reflect inflation rates.[140] His position on ending all federal housing subsidies for cities that enact rent control laws, a current proposal of a number of conservatives and of the real estate lobby, is not known. This kind of adventure in federalism might appeal to him, however, since it would mitigate the effects of what he considers an evil. His support of "right-to-work" laws in the labor field may be analagous. These laws attack the right of contract in making it illegal to establish a union shop; contract has been an important concern of conservatives throughout history. For the sake of hurting unions, however, Friedman and others are willing to make an exception. An invasion of localism, one of Friedman's values, in order to stop rent control may also be seen to be worth it.

On urban environmental questions, Friedman says very little. He does favor developing systems, whenever possible, permitting industries to pollute the environment and then pay for this pollution according to the damages ascertained, a method used in Continental Europe.[141] The small amount of attention given to transportation issues indicates that Friedman has little sympathy for the cause or the costs of government-owned municipal transit systems.[142] All usury laws are opposed; these are antimarket.[143] Any public services jobs scheme, such as CETA, the Comprehensive Employment and Training Act, is regarded as useless and wasteful. Social Security should become a voluntary system, and national health insurance should never be tried.[144] Like some of the libertarian conservatives, Friedman is anticensorship.

The answer to each policy issue is, of course, the market. The market will provide answers to job, housing, transportation, and even educational questions. The market will help to minimize damage to the urban environment. It will determine mass opinion of the quality of the things we read and see, so that censorship of movies or books is neither necessary nor desirable.

Many of us may applaud Friedman on some issues and disagree with him on others. We may like his opposition to censorship, for example, or to drug regulation, labor unions, or the education bureaucracy. Most of his positions embrace an opposition to government intrusions into our lives, and this has a broad appeal, not only to conservatives but to people across the political spectrum.

Reference to the market as the problem-solver for any and all questions is nevertheless simplistic, illogical, and certainly an unproved form of cure-all. The Friedman track-record on fighting inflation in Chile, Israel, and Britain looks bad and can hardly inspire confidence in his perception of the various urban problems he has tackled. Moreover, the hope for a windfall, the penchant for capitalistic adventure, or sheer individual and corporate greed seem like slender and unassuring reeds upon which to build our urban future. Quite to the point of this is Friedman's statement that "All of human experience shows that men love lotteries."[145] Which, in a way, is what Friedman perceives free-market capitalism to be. Then he adds, inaccurately, "Every country that has one makes a profit out of it."[146] Whether this is true or false, however, is not the point; Friedman seems correct in finding much of the essence of the laissez-faire spirit, the twentieth-century version of Adam Smith economics, in the idea of a lottery. And we know how lotteries work—their social results are undesirable, the poor pay for them in greater proportion because of their hope for a victory, the odds are against all of the participants, and, quite often, the game is fixed.

Notes

1. John Kenneth Galbraith, "The Conservative Onslaught," *New York Review of Books* 27 (January 22, 1981): 35.

2. Robert Lekachman, "The Conservative Drift in Modern Economics," in *The New Conservatives: A Critique from the Left*, ed. by Lewis A. Coser and Irving Howe (New York: New American Library, 1976), p. 165.

3. Mary Ellen Leary, "The Property Tax War," *Atlantic Monthly* 241 (May 1978):24.

4. *Wall Street Journal*, January 8, 1981; a letter written in response said, "Laissez-faire may translate to 'Let It Be,' but I expect Milton Friedman might find it a little difficult to 'Imagine No Possessions' "; *Wall Street Journal*, January 22, 1981.

5. Examples: *Wall Street Journal*, November 17, 1977, and January 11, 1980.

6. Milton Friedman and Rose Friedman, *Free to Choose: A Personal Statement* (New York: Harcourt Brace Jovanovich, 1980), p. xi.

7. *Wall Street Journal*, October 24, 1979.

8. "Wrong Number," *Nation* 224 (January 1, 1977): 5.

9. *Wall Street Journal*, August 25, 1980.

10. *Wall Street Journal*, November 17, 1977, and January 11, 1980.

11. Milton Friedman, *From Galbraith to Economic Freedom*, Occasional Paper 49, (London: Institute of Economic Affairs, 1977), p. 11. Some of these titles are: *Essays in Positive Economics* (Chicago: University of Chicago Press, 1953); *A Monetary History of the United States, 1867-1960*, with Anna J. Schwartz (Princeton: Princeton University Press, 1963); and *The Optimum Quantity of Money* (Chicago: Aldine, 1969).

12. Milton Friedman, *Free to Choose: A Personal Statement; Capitalism and Freedom*, with Rose Friedman (Chicago: University of Chicago Press, 1962); *There's No Such Thing as a Free Lunch* (LaSalle, Ill.: Open Court, 1975); *An Economist's Protest: Columns in Political Economy* (New York: Thomas Horton, 1972). These last two reprint some of the same columns and items.

13. Friedman, *From Galbraith to Economic Freedom*, p. 11.

14. Ibid., p. 11.

15. Friedman, *There's No Such Thing as a Free Lunch*, p. 8.

16. Friedman, *Capitalism and Freedom*, p. 197.

17. Friedman, *Free to Choose*, pp. 1-4.

18. Ibid., p. 6.

19. Ibid., p. 7; any Socialist would agree with this point.

20. Ibid., p. 11.

21. Friedman, *There's No Such Thing as a Free Lunch*, p. 31; *Free to Choose*, pp. 1-4.

22. One laudable modern attempt to define these virtues which includes

close attention to the issue of equality is John Rawls, *A Theory of Justice* (Cambridge, Mass.: Belknap Press, 1971).

23. Milton Friedman, "The Role of Monetary Policy," *American Economic Review* 58 (March 1968), pp. 12-14.

24. "Answering the Big Questions," (interview), *Newsweek* (May 29, 1978): 81.

25. Milton Friedman, "Containing Spending," *Society* 14 (March/April 1977): 90.

26. Milton Friedman, "Nobel Lecture: Inflation and Unemployment," *Journal of Political Economy* 85 (June 1977): 451-72.

27. Leary, "The Property Tax War," pp. 20-25; Friedman, *Free to Choose*, pp. 301-5.

28. Galbraith, "The Conservative Onslaught," p. 35.

29. Ibid., p. 34; Burns quoted in *Wall Street Journal,* November 17, 1977; on M-1, a measure of the money supply, Robert H. Parks of Advest, a securities firm, says the "best place" for this mainstay of Friedmanism "is the junkyard"; *Wall Street Journal*, November 17, 1977.

30. *Wall Street Journal*, December 29, 1980.

31. Friedman, "The Role of Monetary Policy," p. 14.

32. Friedman, *Free to Choose,* p. 309.

33. Friedman, *An Economist's Protest: Columns in Political Economy,* p. 143; *Free to Choose,* p. 292.

34. Friedman, *Free to Choose,* p. 298.

35. Friedman, *An Economist's Protest,* p. 167; "Containing Spending," pp. 89-92.

36. Friedman, "Containing Spending," p. 92; *Free to Choose,* pp. 306-7.

37. Friedman, *An Economist's Protest,* p. 167.

38. Friedman, *Free to Choose,* pp. 6, 141, 187-88 (the "educational establishment"), 295, 301; *There's No Such Thing as a Free Lunch,* p. 255.

39. Quoted in Galbraith, "The Conservative Onslaught," p. 31.

40. Friedman, *An Economist's Protest,* p. 34.

41. Quoted in Leary, "The Property Tax War," p. 34.

42. Friedman, *An Economist's Protest,* p. 183.

43. Friedman, *Free to Choose,* pp. ix, x, 299-310.

44. Ibid., pp. 299-300.

45. John Kenneth Galbraith, "The Conservative Onslaught," p. 31; Galbraith believes that "no one, after reflection . . . can conclude that publicly rendered services are less urgently a part of the living

standard than privately purchased ones . . . [and] . . . any general assault on the public services must be understood for what it is; it is an attack on the living standard of the poor,'' pp. 31-32.

46. Friedman, *Free to Choose,* p. 305.

47. *U.S. v Cruikshank,* 92 U.S. 542 (1876); *U.S. v Miller,* 307 U.S. 174 (1939).

48. Friedman, *Free to Choose,* p. 301.

49. Ibid., p. 309.

50. Friedman, *An Economist's Protest,* pp. 31-32.

51. Friedman, *Capitalism and Freedom,* p. 36.

52. Friedman, *An Economist's Protest,* pp. 174-75.

53. Friedman, *Free to Choose,* pp. 305-306.

54. Friedman, *An Economist's Protest,* pp. 118-23, 160-62.

55. Friedman, *There's No Such Thing as a Free Lunch,* p. 32.

56. *Wall Street Journal,* October 24, 1979.

57. Milton Friedman, ''The Free Market and the Energy Crisis,'' *Business and Society Review* 9 (Spring 1974): 86.

58. Friedman, ''The Free Market and the Energy Crisis,'' p. 87.

59. Friedman, *There's No Such Thing as a Free Lunch,* p. 245.

60. Milton Friedman, ''The Uses of Corruption,'' *Newsweek,* March 22, 1976, p. 73.

61. Friedman, *An Economist's Protest,* p. 31.

62. Orlando Letelier, ''The Chicago Boys in Chile,'' *New Statesman* 92 (November 12, 1976): 664.

63. Letelier, ''The Chicago Boys in Chile,'' p. 664.

64. Friedman, *An Economist's Protest,* p. ix.

65. Galbraith, ''The Conservative Onslaught,'' p. 35.

66. Milton Friedman, ''Economic Myths and Public Opinion,'' *Alternative* (Now *American Spectator*) 9 (January 1976): 5-6; *Free to Choose,* p. 5.

67. Milton Friedman, ''Myths That Keep People Hungry,'' *Harpers* 234 (January-June 1967): 16-24; ''Containing Spending,'' p. 90; *Free to Choose,* pp. 100-1; *Capitalism and Freedom,* p. 97.

68. Friedman, *Capitalism and Freedom,* pp. 116-17, 132; also, see *An Economist's Protest,* p. 202.

69. Friedman, *Free to Choose,* p. xiii.

70. 277 U.S. 479 (1928).

71. Friedman, *Free to Choose,* p. xiii; on the amusing point of Professor Friedman's ties, see *Wall Street Journal,* January 27, 1981.

72. Friedman, ''Containing Spending,'' p. 89.

73. Friedman, *Free to Choose,* p. 5.

74. Friedman, "Containing Spending," p. 89.

75. "The Growing Burden of State Taxes," *Consumers Research* 64 (February 1981): 15-19.

76. Friedman, "Containing Spending," p. 91.

77. Friedman, *Free to Choose,* p. 37.

78. Duncan Campbell, "A Secret Plan for Dictatorship," *New Statesman* 100 (December 2, 1980): 8-9, 12.

79. Friedman, *Capitalism and Freedom,* p. 4.

80. Friedman, "Containing Spending," p. 89.

81. Friedman, *Free to Choose,* p. 110.

82. Friedman, *There's No Such Thing as a Free Lunch,* pp. 9-10; *An Economist's Protest,* pp. 130, 165-66.

83. Friedman, *There's No Such Thing as a Free Lunch,* p. 10.

84. Ibid., pp. 27, 110.

85. Friedman, *Free to Choose,* pp. 101-2; *There's No Such Thing as a Free Lunch,* p. 27.

86. Friedman, *Free to Choose,* pp. 33, 119; *There's No Such Thing as a Free Lunch,* p. 21; *An Economist's Protest,* 213.

87. Friedman, *An Economist's Protest,* pp. 205-7.

88. Ibid., p. 207; *Capitalism and Freedom,* p. 190.

89. Friedman, *Free to Choose,* pp. 101-2; "Containing Spending," p. 90.

90. Friedman, *An Economist's Protest,* p. 160.

91. "Government can't have a responsibility any more than . . . business can"; *There's No Such Thing as a Free Lunch,* p. 247.

92. Friedman, *There's No Such Thing as a Free Lunch,* p. 245; *Capitalism and Freedom,* pp. 132-35; *An Economist's Protest,* pp. 177-82.

93. Friedman, *Capitalism and Freedom,* pp. 132, 135-56.

94. Friedman, *There's No Such Thing as a Free Lunch,* p. 241.

95. Friedman, *An Economist's Protest,* p. 150; for another view, see John Kenneth Galbraith, "Was Ford a Fraud?" in his *The Liberal Hour* (Boston: Houghton Mifflin, 1960), pp. 141-65.

96. Friedman, *There's No Such Thing as a Free Lunch,* pp. 36-37.

97. Friedman, *Capitalism and Freedom,* p. 21.

98. Friedman, *An Economist's Protest,* p. 151.

99. Friedman, *Capitalism and Freedom,* pp. 109, 110, 111-15.

100. Ibid., p. 116.

101. Ibid., pp. 117, 118.

102. Friedman, *Free to Choose,* p. 128.

103. Friedman, *An Economist's Protest,* p. 205.

104. Friedman, *Free to Choose*, pp. 39, 145.

105. Ibid., p. 141.

106. Leary, "The Property Tax War," pp. 20-25; *An Economist's Protest*, p. 160.

107. Friedman, *An Economist's Protest*, p. 160.

108. Ibid., *An Economist's Protest*, p. 69.

109. Friedman, "How to Save the Housing Industry," *Newsweek*, May 26, 1980, p. 80; *Free to Choose*, p. 309.

110. Friedman, *An Economist's Protest*, pp. 132-40; *Free to Choose*, pp. 120-27; *There's No Such Thing as a Free Lunch*, pp. 30, 206-7.

111. Friedman, *An Economist's Protest*, pp. 132-40; *Free to Choose*, pp. 120-27.

112. Friedman, *An Economist's Protest*, p. 139.

113. Friedman, *Free to Choose*, p. 125. These criteria originated with Martin Anderson, now an adviser on domestic policy to President Reagan.

114. Robert Lekachman, *Economists at Bay: Why the Experts Will Never Solve Your Problems* (New York: McGraw-Hill, 1976), pp. 64-69.

115. Friedman, *An Economist's Protest*, p. 30.

116. Friedman, *Free to Choose*, p. 154.

117. Friedman, *There's No Such Thing as a Free Lunch*, p. 89.

118. Friedman, *An Economist's Protest*, p. 190.

119. Ibid., pp. 190-91; *Free to Choose*, pp. 162-75.

120. Friedman, *Free to Choose*, pp. 162-75.

121. Friedman, *An Economist's Protest*, p. 190.

122. Friedman, *There's No Such Thing as a Free Lunch*, p. 92.

123. Friedman, *An Economist's Protest*, pp. 217-19.

124. Ibid., p. 195.

125. Ibid.

126. Friedman, *Free to Choose*, p. 162.

127. Christopher Jencks quoted in Lekachman, in *Economists at Bay*, p. 153.

128. Ibid.

129. Friedman, *An Economist's Protest*, p. 187.

130. Friedman, *Free to Choose*, p. 68; of course, most of the "chilling effects" in higher education in our recent history have come from the political Right.

131. Friedman, *An Economist's Protest*, pp. 191-92.

132. Friedman, *There's No Such Thing as a Free Lunch*, p. 10.

133. Friedman, *Free to Choose*, p. 223.

134. Ibid., pp. 228-47.

135. Ibid., p. 243.

136. Friedman, *Capitalism and Freedom,* p. 116; *Free to Choose,* p. 246.

137. Friedman, *Capitalism and Freedom,* pp. 180-81; *An Economist's Protest,* pp. 144-45; *There's No Such Thing as a Free Lunch,* pp. 6-7.

138. Friedman, *An Economist's Protest,* p. 144.

139. Friedman, *Free to Choose,* pp. 109-11; *An Economist's Protest,* pp. 157-58; *Capitalism and Freedom,* pp. 178-80; *There's No Such Thing as a Free Lunch,* pp. 249-50.

140. Friedman, "How to Save the Housing Industry," p. 80.

141. Friedman, *There's No Such Thing as a Free Lunch,* p. 16.

142. Friedman, "The Free Market and the Energy Crisis," p. 87; "Economic Myths and Public Opinion," p. 8.

143. Friedman, *An Economist's Protest,* p. 154.

144. Friedman, *Free to Choose,* pp. 112-15; "Social Security: The Poor Man's Welfare Payment to the Middle Class," *Washington Monthly* 4 (May 1972), pp. 11-16; quoted in *Wall Street Journal,* January 11, 1980; *An Economist's Protest*, pp. 131-32.

145. Friedman, *An Economist's Protest,* p. 153.

146. Friedman, "The Free Market and the Energy Crisis," p.87.

5

IRVING KRISTOL:
THE CITY OF DISCONTENTS

Irving Kristol has been called America's "quintessential neo-conservative," for he is closely associated with that group of influential intellectuals—Daniel Bell, Norman Podhoretz, Daniel Patrick Mohnihan, Nathan Glazer, and Seymour M. Lipset, among others.[1] He could very well be characterized as its founder (as well as the co-founder of the journals *Encounter* and *The Public Interest*), and he is the only member of that sturdy band who does not object to being known as a "neo-conservative."[2]

Any serious attempt to chart and anticipate the policies of a City of the Right must take neoconservatism, and particularly its great exponent, into account. The neoconservatives are the most influential of the shadings of the Right upon the thinking of policy makers in both of the major political parties; and among these influentials, Irving Kristol has written about the cities and their problems more provocatively than any other person. His influence, moreover, is direct: he was an adviser to President Ronald Reagan during the 1980 campaign, and he will surely be heard in policy councils in the coming years. Kristol is therefore a natural choice for this study, mostly for reasons of his influence and attention to urban issues. But he is also important because he recognizes the potential of ideas and can organize his journals, institutes, associates, and study groups to promote these ideas so that they have maximum impact.

It seems likely that Kristol's appreciation of the power of ideas can be owed to his early Marxist—and, more precisely, Trotskyist—experience. Trotskyists, like all groups of the radical Left, are well aware that the Russian Revolution was a product of the ideas of Marx and Lenin as much as it was of anything else. Although he was a Trotskyist only through his years at the City College of New York in the late 1930s, Kristol did assume an active role at that time in the Young Peoples Socialist League (YPSL). Trotskyists at that time were of course appalled at Stalin's betrayal of the Russian Revolution, his emphasis upon the primacy of the Soviet Union and its interests above all other considerations, his pact with Hitler, and his purge trials. In examining their positions on these and other questions, however, they tended to split hairs and to break up into even smaller factions and organizations. Their debates were hot, but they also emphasized logical consistency, ideological purity, and the ongoing dialectical processes of history and of debate. Kristol's writings today can be said, on most occasions, to show a striving for these emphases. The Trotskyists also worried about the myths swallowed by the public; Kristol's positions reflect this, particularly his dislike of Populist traditions and influence. Perhaps most of all, the Trotskyists worried about their theory facing up to the dangers and opportunities posed by events. Kristol's works certainly exhibit a similar preoccupation.[3]

Besides being the Jesuits of the Left, the Trotskyists of the 1930s can be fairly said to be prone to a "take-over" syndrome. For reasons that were never too clear, they wished to infiltrate various organizations and bring them over to the Trotskyist "line." Kristol is much too shrewd to believe in such crude and invariably unsuccessful schemes. He nevertheless has a driving ambition and zealotry that carry him far, not only in his editing, but also in organizing efforts—symposia, special issues devoted to a given topic, an institute, or even a new journal. And a "take-over" of sorts has occurred as a result of his activities, one that is far beyond the imaginings of any Trotskyist dream. Irving Kristol is at the center of the most listened to, most persuasive, and best-placed group of intellectuals in America—the neoconservatives. He can influence policy and opinion as a member of the Board of Contributors to the *Wall Street Journal,* as a performer on the lecture circuit, as a scholar-in-residence at the American Enterprise Institute of Policy Research in Washington, D.C., and as editor of the small-circulation but highly influential *Public Interest* magazine.[4]

Kristol was born in New York City on January 22, 1920. He received a Phi Beta Kappa key with his B.A. degree from City College of New York (CCNY) in 1940, and this is the only degree he has ever sought. (He received an honorary LL.D. from Franklin and Marshall College in 1972.) He gave up his socialism early, turning in his YPSL card before joining the Army in World War II.[5] Reflecting upon his change of heart, Kristol says,

> There was nothing mysterious or sinister about this transition. I ceased being a radical or a socialist because . . . I concluded that political radicalism was, more often than not, inherently self-defeating and that socialism—in any meaningful sense of that term—was intrinsically utopian. At first I reached this conclusion with some reluctance and regret. In retrospect, however, I am pleased that I reached it when I did.[6]

This was not so remarkable a change when it is remembered that most of Kristol's friends from his CCNY days, people who are not great jewels in the neoconservative diadem, were embarking, at roughly the same time, upon the path which would take them steadily rightward as well.

Nathan Glazer, one of the most prominent of these, recalls his early work with Kristol, right after the war, in the offices of *Commentary* magazine. Glazer feels that it is significant that Kristol, unlike his contemporaries, exhibited a marked interest in religion, and especially in Judaism, in those days.[7] Kristol today emphasizes the decline of religion in American life, most particularly the loss of belief in a life after death, as a leading cause of our malaise.[8] At that early point in his career, Glazer notes, young Irving, again unlike his close associates, demonstrated an acute interest in business, business people, speculation, the money market, and money itself.[9] Kristol's writing today is often concerned with the economy and with the theme of justifying capitalism to the poor, to the world, and to himself.[10]

The postwar years were of course cold war years, and the menace of McCarthyism was abroad in the land. It was a time of trial for civil libertarians of all political persuasions, and the truth is that Kristol did not stand up to the test very well. Particularly controversial was a 1952 *Commentary* article on Senator Joseph McCarthy that concluded: "There is one thing that the American people know about Senator McCarthy: he, like them, is unequivocally anti-Communist. About the spokesmen for American liberalism, they know no such thing."[11] Kristol has had to bear the burden of having this article thrown in his face from time to time, but he explains himself by saying that the senator from Wisconsin had achieved popularity because the liberals, especially in academia, had given the people little reason to think that they could distinguish Communists and their spies from "authentic" liberals, radicals, and social democrats.[12]

Irving Howe, a fellow leftist of CCNY days who did not become a neoconservative but instead chose the path of democratic socialism, states that Kristol was not pro-Joe McCarthy, but that he was too often on the attack against anti-McCarthy people at that time. Clearly, according to Howe, the danger was McCarthy, not the people attacked by Kristol.[13] The article in question, its closing quotation, Howe's statement, and the activities of Kristol at the time suggest that Kristol did not rise to the occasion as astutely as most civil libertarians might be expected to; what is more, we have clear evidence that Kristol was moving to the other side of the political spectrum at this crucial time. For Irving Kristol, as for so many others (including Presidents Nixon and Reagan) the response to the McCarthy years has proved to be a prophetic indicator of a certain political path.

Whether Kristol is guilty of being too kind to McCarthy—or, more accurately, too unkind to McCarthy's critics and detractors— there seems to be little question about his involvement in a rather sordid affair with an entity called the American Committee for Cultural Freedom. The ACCF, with which Kristol was closely connected for several years and for whom he served as executive secretary, was a funnel for CIA funds to Kristol's London-based magazine, *Encounter*. The integrity of *Encounter* and, for that matter, Kristol, was brought into question by the revelation of CIA funding in the early 1960s. Whether Kristol knowingly was working as an agent of the CIA is conjectural, but the evidence shows clearly that he was not uninvolved and that he showed no principalled opposition to the arrangement at any time.[14]

The years have given Kristol some hard brickbats, but he has also received almost obsequious praise. Kristol receives frequent accolades not only from his neoconservative colleagues, but from other people on the Right: William F. Buckley, Jr., Edward C. Banfield, and Emmett Tyrrell, for example. His is a distinguished career, one that has seen the founding of *The Public Interest,* a great spate of articles and essays (technically speaking, Kristol has never written one complete book, only collections of his short pieces), and his present appointment with the business-sponsored American Enterprise Institute for Policy Research. Before this appointment, there was a span of years as Henry Luce Professor of Urban Values at New York University, which, when one thinks about it, is not without its ironies. One commentator, knowing what Kristol thinks about urban values, said that it was "for all the world like putting W. C. Fields in charge of a children's day care center."[15] It is a perceptive remark, for Kristol is the most specifically anti-urban, both in temperament and in policy terms, of any of the five principals chosen for this study.

Kristol's Neoconservatism

Kristol's brand of conservatism is neoconservatism, which he sees as a set of principles generally supported by all of the well-known neoconservative architects. In terms of American domestic policy, there are four major principles.

First, there is acceptance of the welfare state. It is perfectly legitimate for the state to help people deal with the problems of unemployment, infirmity, and age. The difficulty is with the Great Society version of the welfare state—the ambitious programs to eradicate poverty, to transfer income from one group of people to another when this does not seem necessary, and to promote and subsidize the polarization of groups. Kristol regards this approach as a plan for a paternalistic state rather than a welfare state.

Next, there is a great respect for the economic forces of the marketplace. Neoconservatives may tinker with the market for some great social purpose, but they eschew, wherever possible, the imposition of bureaucratic controls.

Third, says Kristol, neoconservatives respect such traditional values and institutions as religion, the family, and the "high culture" of Western civilization. The other side of this coin, as one might expect, is a thorough rejection of the counter culture that has played such an important role in America over the past two decades. Indeed, the so-called values of the counterculture are seen as anathema.

Finally, neoconservatives strongly favor equality of opportunity, but reject all socialist-style leveling and egalitarian ideas that insist upon "equal shares of everything."[16]

These four features of the faith hardly define neoconservatism adequately. Perhaps the best succinct definition is that it is an "intellectual party" devoted to the legitimation and promotion of certain policies and institutions.[17] Many of the leading neoconservatives, and most certainly Kristol, are politically active. They advise political figures in government and during campaigns. One of the foremost neoconservative thinkers, Daniel Patrick Moynihan, became a senator from New York in 1976 after holding several high government positions in the Nixon and Johnson administrations. Neoconservatives are centered in elite universities and research institutes, and they have honeycombed virtually all of the major foundations. These neoconservatives get plenty of attention from the media (despite their frequent criticism of the media as lopsidedly liberal) or they *are* the media, producing columns, essays, or opinion pieces. They are especially evident in the little journals of opinion—*Harpers* or *The New Leader* are good examples—either as contributors or as subjects of controversy. And, in the center of all of these activities, two journals—*Commentary* and Kristol's own *Public Interest*—stand out as the locus and focus of neoconservatism.[18]

Other views of neoconservatism, however, do not necessarily support some of these descriptions. Robert Bartley, writing in the journal that later became *The American Spectator*, does not believe that legitimation of institutions or of policies is their major function:

> The basic viewpoint of the group rests on its conception of society. A society, culture or civilization is held together not ultimately by its formal institutions but by informal things—traditions, values, feelings, and expectations shared by its citizens. . . . [19]

Neoconservatism is not so much about government, policies, or institutions; it is about society, the individuals who make up society, and the bonds and common goals held by people. The social contract is between individuals, not between people and government. Neoconservatism thus excludes all plans aimed at the betterment of human nature and all utopianism. It is pragmatic even though it possesses those ideals of "traditions, values, feelings, and expectations." It is unsentimental, even bitter. "I define a neo-conservative," says Kristol, "as a liberal who has been mugged by reality."[20]

This bitterness may stem from the ashes-in-the-mouth feeling left by his unsatisfying years of liberalism. Like all prominent neoconservatives, Kristol is very harsh with liberalism. It has two parts today, he says:

> First, it entails ever-greater governmental intervention in certain areas—economics, educational administration, the electoral process, etc.—to achieve greater equality, itself now identified with "true liberty." Second, it entails less governmental intervention in those areas—religion, school curricula, culture, entertainment, etc.—which have to do with the formation of character, and in which it is assumed that "the marketplace of ideas" will "naturally" produce ideal results.[21]

Liberalism is therefore a combination of "moralistic egalitarianism" and "optimistic 'permissiveness.' "[22] He also points out

that many people who are regarded as liberals—John Kenneth
Galbraith and Michael Harrington are cases in point—are
actually admitted socialists.

Just as Kristol's view of liberalism helps to further define
his neoconservatism, so does his view of conservatism—conservatism
in its more pristine form—give us insight:

> (These) sentiments . . . are at the root of conservative
> virtue: a dogged loyalty to a traditional way of life;
> an intellectual aversion to innovation based on mere theoretical
> speculation; and a sense of having a fiduciary relation to the
> whole nation—past, present, and future. . . . There is
> always a kind of immunity to fashionable political ideas
> which is associated with conservatism, and a country that
> does not have a goodly portion of it is incapable of
> stable and orderly government. No political system can
> endure without engendering, in a perfectly organic way,
> this kind of conservat[ism]. . . . It is the antibody of the
> body politic.[23]

In addition, conservatives believe, according to Kristol, that
institutions that have survived for a long period of time have
a reason and purpose for existing, an inherent wisdom that may
escape the purview of a "rational" observer. Our inability to
adequately explain or defend such institutions is not a defect
in them, but a defect in us. Most people, says Kristol, can feel
the force of this argument intuitively if not intellectually. Peoples'
instincts are, after all, mostly conservative.[24]

Many institutions exist for long periods of time, however,
which are not so justifiable. Slavery and serfdom are examples.
But this is not the point. The point is that while Kristol is
clearly a neoconservative, he is also, in many respects, a plain
old conservative. He is just more pragmatic, more in tune with
the times, than conservatives of a more classic genre. He will
be glad to tell anyone that such adamant conservatism as that of
the New Right, or of the Moral Majority, or even of William
F. Buckley, Jr., tends to run off in all directions and is
therefore not very productive.[25] Many agree with him. Peter

Steinfels, one of the foremost writers on neoconservatism, indicates this when he says that neoconservatism is the serious conservatism that America has lacked for so long.[26]

Kristol does not view neoconservatism as a static, nor as a *status quo*, doctrine. He likes to call himself a conservative reformer, even though his writings usually take up the cudgels against reformers.[27] Since he is pragmatic, he also regards himself as anti-ideological. Writing with his neoconservative colleague, Daniel Bell, in the first issue of *The Public Interest*, Kristol pointed out that "a prior commitment to an ideology, whether it be liberal, conservative or radical . . . causes one to *preconceive* reality; and it is exactly such preconceptions that are the worst hindrances to knowing-what-one-is-talking-about."[28] It suffices, at this point, to note that Kristol's neoconservative viewpoint is consistently heavy with strong ideological components, preferences, and predispositions.

In this "anti-ideological" vein can be found Irving Kristol's "law of unintended consequences," which is more of a truism than a law of politics. Stated briefly, it is the notion that today's solution to a problem is tomorrow's dilemma.[29] This is hardly a profound truth, yet the post-World War II years have shown its application to a host of urban policies ranging from urban renewal to welfare programs to health and transportation policies. Kristol is merely reminding us of a factor that appears to be an inevitable consequence of policymaking.

What Kristol's "law of unintended consequences" ultimately points out is the limited ability of all empirical endeavors in policymaking and, for that matter, in social science. This is interesting because his neoconservatism is really a blend of the use of empirical data generated by a variety of think tanks, universities, and government agencies with an Aristotelian concern with values.[30] (A political scientist might call it a Leo Straussian concern with values.) Neoconservatism may be the first conservative political framework established in America to incorporate this blend, although Kristol seems less likely than some of his cohorts to rely on empirical data.[31]

Reliance upon such data and upon the methods involved in its use fails to keep Kristol and his colleagues from adopting a sweeping, all too confident, and careless approach in setting out premises and conclusions. This is apparently a chronic occupational disease of neoconservatism. One writer charitably calls it a "knowing" approach.[32] A couple of examples from Kristol's work will demonstrate this characteristic:

> Human talents and abilities . . . distribute themselves along a bell-shaped curve, with most people clustered around the middle and with much smaller percentages at the lower and higher ends . . . [another] demonstrable fact is that in all modern bourgeois societies, the distribution of income is also along a bell-shaped curve. . . . [33]

This statement requires little comment; there are as many sets of statistics to refute the first "curve" as there are to dispute the latter. Kristol gets even more carried away when he predicts:

> A fair proportion of the academic community would surely look more benevolently on a new college whose curriculum made ample provision for instruction in the theory of guerrilla warfare than one that made a knowledge of classical political philosophy compulsory.[34]

Numerous examples of such mad ravings and hyperbolic drivel detract mightily from Kristol's work. The often hasty and reckless approach which accounts for them also calls into question the supposed empirical bias of his conclusions. Many disconcerting and careless references and passages appear in his essays as well, indicating, for example, the total failure of the Swedish and British welfare systems as if this was a carefully documented and agreed-upon premise, which, of course, is not the case.[35]

"Empiricism, who cares about that?" Kristol would probably reply. His goal is not to achieve some rarefied kind of social science sophistication, but to achieve the neoconservative goals of restoring control to society, eliminating a lot of wasteful bureaucracy and regulation, and, above all, establishing and promoting a republican sensibility in our citizenry, warning us of the counter cultural dangers along the way. These goals can be reached—or they cannot, depending on whether Kristol is in an optimistic or apocalyptic mood. He seems to fluctuate between these two poles a great deal of the time.

Whatever his mood, he believes in the virtues of capitalism, for they are intimately tied to the virtues of republican self-government. In a word, money is freedom, and freedom is what a political culture is all about. In a quotation reminiscent of similar ones by Buckley and Friedman, the venerable leader of neoconservatism states that "material prosperity is not something to sneer at. Money is freedom to the degree that with money you have power, to the degree that with power you are free from coercion."[36]

The Founding Fathers knew this, says Kristol, and they intended this to be a capitalist nation. They recognized its strong link with liberty in the formation and continuation of a limited and republican government. The American Revolution was not a class revolution in the sense of 1789 France or 1917 Russia. It was a bourgeois revolution that, unlike others, did not promise the abolition of poverty. It sought instead, and successfully, to maximize the chance to escape poverty by establishing a system to promote economic growth and the welfare of all. Economic growth is seen by Kristol, and by all of the neoconservatives, as the surest and most efficient way of combatting poverty.[37] Capitalism promises, and delivers, a continuous improvement in the material well-being of all citizens and, at the same time, it promises an unprecedented and unique individual freedom for all.[38]

Kristol, then, is enthusiastic about capitalism because it provides political freedom as well as an important measure of economic freedom. The virtues of the marketplace are far-reaching. Whether he is perceptive in doing so, he appears to be right in saying that the typical justifications for capitalism today are the Protestant work ethic, Social Darwinism as a kind of superiority of the fittest that is akin to racism, and the need to promote and protect technology and the elite who manage this technology.[39] Though he recognizes that attempts to rationalize the system are to a great extent facile and certainly incomplete, he is not going to assume the role of questioner or iconoclast. He accepts, even glorifies, the modern corporation, despite all its limitations. It is practical to do so. The criterion is, what works? And the answer is capitalism and the modern corporation.

Obviously, some people are not participants in this array of opportunities and all these material benefits. Poverty persists. The demands of society persist; yet many of these demands, Kristol says, are unreasonable. The demands, whether they are just or unjust, result from societal frustration: "the overwhelming majority of the people lead lives of considerable frustration and if society is to endure, it needs to be able to rely on a goodly measure of stoical resignation."[40] That's right—stoical resignation. We need more of it, though it, like everything else, does not have to be shared equally.

Stoical resignation is one of the virtues of a society governed by a republican system and a republican sensibility. There is, indeed, something that can be called "republican virtue" while, alas, there is no such entity as "democratic virtue."[41] Kristol often quotes Michael Oakeshott's belief that the function of government is to "tend to the arrangements of society."[42] Free people do not hold a social contract or covenant with their government or with any political leaders; the contract is between and among themselves. And since the satisfactions of private life are far superior to those of any political life, the relationship of the "good life" to politics is quite obvious to Kristol. Avoid utopian schemes, for all of them are "pernicious."[43] Concentrate instead on providing and preserving that important "social space" to which the market is so congenial and within which civil and political liberty can flower.[44] This is a bourgeois ideal, to be sure, but it is seen by Kristol as the only path by which humankind can hope to avoid tyranny.

Capitalism, along with its benefits and defects, is therefore an absolutely necessary condition in Kristol's neoconservative world of the present and hope for the future. The issue of capitalism's preservation, moreover, does not depend upon the strong empirical evidence of its good economic performance. That matter has long been decided in its favor. The trouble is with the ethos of capitalism.[45] (Again, Kristol eschews what seems to be the empirical for the sake of his intuitive feelings.) Capitalism's continuation into the future will depend upon the virtue, reason, and yes, stoical resignation of the people. The people will determine the kind of society we live in, and Kristol emphasizes this view in several of his essays. This may sound simplistic, and it certainly has no truck with "elite rule" theorists, but Kristol believes it to be the unspoken issue of American politics and civilization. Very few politicians go around asking whether the people are virtuous or trustworthy. As Jimmy Carter and others have shown, the tendency is quite the opposite. The Founding Fathers were different. They worried about the people and their tendencies, Kristol tells us, and for good reason. They recognized that self-government meant self-discipline. Unfortunately, Kristol notes, today "we tend to take it for granted that all expressions of *material* grievances by the people must be basically legitimate."[46] And our assumption, most of the time, is that once these material grievances are satisfied, the goodness of people will reassert itself. Such a view is wholly impractical and wrong. Is this mean-spirited? What about faith in the people?

> I do indeed have faith in the common people—only I don't have very much faith in them. . . . I include myself among those common people and, knowing myself as I do, I would say that anyone who constructed a political system based on unlimited faith in my good character was someone with a fondness for high-risk enterprise. To put it another way: the common man is not a fool, and the proof that he is not a fool is that he has such modest faith in himself.[47]

The main difficulty is not with Kristol, nor with his neoconservative colleagues, nor with most of the people, whose instincts are conservative, he says, anyway. It is with the counterculture and its apologists, that ragtag, uncouth, irreverent, and uncaring bunch of barbarians who continue to carry the torch of the spirit of the 1960s. These people have caused that which exists to be vulnerable for no other reason than it exists.Sustaining or reforming things has become passé.[48] Like Banfield, Kristol believes that television is also to blame. "The revolution of rising expectations" causes people to think that "to see something on television is to feel entitled to it."[49] Never mind that this condition serves the very intents and purposes of capitalism.

The problem is that nothing in our urbanized and democratized culture is sacred or revered; at the same time, the people, those people who really cannot be trusted, are spiritually sick, and they are looking around for a "patent medicine of the soul."[50] Populism, that unthinking set of grass-roots attitudes that is well mixed with the cries of unreason and bigotry, has always been present in the American political culture. It can be awakened anytime, turning the public into a great beast. The common man may have good sense, but he is alienated today perhaps as never before, and he is not powerless.[51] So Kristol, like his neoconservative colleagues, worries a great deal.

This neoconservative view of society does not always obtain. Kristol is quite inconsistent when he talks about the people. For tactical reasons, he will use them against the government, against the counterculture, or against any straw man he may be debating.[52] He then speaks of their enlightened down-to-earth good sense, their devotion to the conservation of energy resources, or their awareness of matters that conventional wisdom deems them unaware. All the same, the purpose of analyzing Kristol's thought could not be fulfilled if this praise for the masses was taken very seriously. Like conservatives of all stripes, Kristol would rather keep the people at arms' length and view them through his elite lens.

The heart of this problem with the people is that we live in an urban civilization with urban discontents, and this state of affairs, states Kristol, is starkly at odds with our history and, more importantly, with any hope of maintaining republican virtue. An urban civilization is a *democratic* civilization, and that is unfortunate. Democratic civilization, when used as a term by Kristol, means "mob" civilization—and these last two words can hardly be said to be compatible.[53] This kind of decadent "mob society" is not capable of much except its own destruction. The absence of republican virtue means that we are being overtaken by a lack of any sense of political, social, or moral obligation, that we no longer possess any sense of stoic resignation, and that we are immune to civilized sensibilities as we join popular fads and are swayed by tides of opinion. Indeed, the very principle of authority no longer "makes sense" to people.[54] The Founding Fathers anticipated these problems. They did not want an urban civilization; they were adamantly opposed to one.

Kristol's neoconservatism is therefore specifically and openly anti-urban. Capitalism and republicanism and their virtues, which are prized and praised as the ways to manage a government and an economy, are placed in jeopardy by an urban civilization, by this unfettered democracy, and by the "mob" state of mind that they foster and encourage. One can only wonder why Kristol would accept a post as professor of urban values in the first place.

Kristol's Anti-Urban Vision

Irving Kristol has lived in old, big cities all his life—London, Washington, and more than any place, New York—and he prefers them over any other environment. Yet he takes what can only be considered an unsympathetic view towards them, their people, and their problems. This would be more easily understood if, like Buckley, he stood aloof from the city, perhaps in it but never of it. Kristol apparently likes the city personally, but he dislikes urban civilization intensely. It serves his needs but not the needs of society.

The reasons for this somewhat anomalous set of attitudes are fathomable if we explore his view, his vision—or, if you will, his perspective on urban America. This perspective entails questions about the values and purposes of cities and of urban civilization in America, the historical interpretation proffered by Kristol on how the cities have evolved to their present state, and, above all, his belief that an urban "new class" has shaped not only the policies and life of our cities, but of the nation as well.

That America could very well get along without its big cities is self-evident to Kristol. Cities are no longer the commercial, financial, technological, cultural or transportation centers they once were; therefore, "It is conceivable . . . that, though our major cities keep floundering in a sea of troubles, the nation as a whole will not be profoundly affected."[55] In any event, it is clear that most people prefer not to live in them; but for those who do there is now a strong preference for cities like Los Angeles, Houston, or Tucson—cities that embrace a suburban life-style—rather than for places like New York, Philadelphia, Cleveland, or Detroit.[56] The urban crisis which the nation is presently experiencing is said, inaccurately, to be limited in scope, limited in fact to only seventeen Northeastern and Midwestern cities. The remainder of our cities, imperfect though they may be, are faced with no particularly overwhelming problems.[57]

The truth is that many Sun Belt and Western cities face the very problems that have plagued urban centers of the Northeast and Midwest—the loss of industry, jobs, and population, deteriorating schools and public services, crime, environmental pollution, and racial and ethnic tensions. Even if such inaccuracies are put aside, Kristol's other feckless statements cannot be allowed to pass. Kristol overlooks, or chooses to ignore, the uniqueness of America's older and bigger cities and their special contributions to our life and culture. Their many market specializations permit people who live outside them, as well as residents, to shop at good bookstores, enjoy the flavors of ethnic life, or to seek out special products and services unobtainable elsewhere. Then there is their high culture. True, one can have culture in the suburbs and rural areas, but not a Metropolitan Opera, a Boston Symphony, or a Tyrone Guthrie Theatre Center. Kristol admits this when he says that both the high and the low of civilization is bred in the cities.[58] And the unique individuality of our large cities is further illustrated by the difficulty one has in generalizing about them. This difficulty has bothered urban specialists and students of urban government and policy for a long time, and even Kristol might admit that this is a problem. Even though all generalization in urban studies is difficult, however, it can be said that the task is at least slightly easier when we talk or write about small or medium-sized cities or, even with their admittedly great diversity, the suburbs. Our great cities are great treasures, a great national resource, and their misuse and abuse does not justify dismissing them from our concern and consideration.

Kristol believes that whatever we think about our old, great cities, their problems are intractable. A whole set of trends works against solving them: the decline of the railroads, containerization in the shipping industry, the end of manufacturing in the cities, the movement of corporate headquarters from the cities, and the rise of university towns as cultural centers. No reversals of these trends are expected, and so the cities can be expected to continue to decline. Let them, says Kristol. We can all make adjustments accordingly. He believes, in fact, that no other course is possible and that one of the chief shortcomings of much urban analysis is the failure to realize this.[59]

The problem, then, is not so much with the cities. *It is with us.* Any environmentalist will immediately recognize this as "Pogoism." Kristol even goes to the length of quoting the little possum of the comic strips directly, saying that we have met the enemy and it is us.[60] Such banality gets us nowhere. If we succeed in generalizing a problem or a condition to the point at which we are all responsible for it (and, it is suggested, *equally* responsible as well) then it becomes apparent that no one is responsible. Environmentalists are used to this ploy and recognize that it leads to paralysis rather than action. Those devoted to the urban cause may see it used more often in the future.

Kristol views this urban problem in large part as due to a perverse "urban mentality: irreverent, speculative, pleasure-loving, self-serving, belligerent toward all conventional pieties" and incompatible with republican survival. He believes that this mindset has existed throughout the history of big cities and has always made them bad places, totally lacking in civic virtue. Small and mid-sized cities have always been more governable and more manageable, but public officials, planners, and social scientists alike have been puzzled and dismayed by the quandaries of big-city governance. To day, they continuously shift—from patronage to merit systems and back again, from metropolitan amalgamation or federation to neighborhood control and back again—displaying, to Kristol's mind, a certain trendiness, but no sure grip of governance and the problems of governance.[61] They fail to recognize, Kristol asserts, that the real crisis of the cities is the absence of bourgeois values.[62]

Large cities and their citizens have never respected bourgeois values, even though these values, which entail civic virtue and a sense of political and social obligation, are the bedrock of a republic. The American city was saved from itself in the nineteenth century because a great deal of technological innovation took place which supposedly made up for some of these missing sensibilities. An urban mentality was in evidence, but America's saving grace was that it was limited to the cities.

All of this has now changed, and for the worse. Today, because of mass education and mass communications, America has become an urban civilization. It does not matter whether we live in small towns, the hinterland, or the cities, for we are all incorporated into this mass phenomenon. This is unprecedented in human history, and it presents us, according to Kristol, with a special problem. America has always been able to exist and progress as a republic in spite of her cities because the perverse urban mentality has been confined. Now it is pervasive. The result is that we find the democratic ethos, the "mob" mentality of the city, spilling over into the countryside and into the length and breadth of the land. The counter culture is everywhere, and no one can hide from it.[63]

Five major experiences are now shared by all Americans, urban, rural, or suburban, and these five experiences send "shivers of foreboding" through Kristol and through the body politic. These are: 1) the technological imperative, or the need for technology in order for us to survive; 2) the revolution of rising expectations, which is making people "determinedly unreasonable" and given to selfishness and self-indulgence; 3) the generation gap; 4) our changing popular culture and the rise of counter culture; and 5) the decline of religion, which Kristol sees as the most profound change of all.[64] The outlook, under these pressures, is not reassuring.

> One wonders: how can a bourgeois society survive in a cultural ambience that derides every traditional bourgeois virtue and celebrates promiscuity, homosexuality, drugs, political terrorism—anything, in short, that is in bourgeois eyes perverse?[65]

There are some oddities that are a part of this transformation of American bourgeois culture into an urban "mob" mentality. One is the corruption, to which Kristol alludes in several of his pieces, wrought by the country's material prosperity. It has fed a complacency as well as the economic independence of many undesirable social critics. If corruption of this sort has occurrred, it must be asked, is not capitalism, which Kristol so earnestly defends, a root cause? An even greater paradox is Kristol's assertion that we are experiencing the life of an urban civilization *without cities*. The true cities of the world, he believes, are those cities like London, Paris, Rome, or Vienna, that incorporate all of the vital centers of national life—cultural, political, economic, and financial. Americans have never had such a city. He believes that we have a political capital, a financial center, some steel-producing centers, an automobile city, oil cities, a meat-marketing center. We *use* our cities and often abuse them in the process, but in the main, they are viewed simply—unlike the great European cities—as fulfillments of our pragmatic, utilitarian goals.[66] This is an intrinsically interesting description of American cities, and there is assuredly some point in knowing where we have been in our urban past. As an historical analysis, it is a bit overdone, all the same, and it may be (let us hope it is not) in accord with the urban spirit of the 1980s.

Assuming that Kristol is right, just how have we become a civilization devoted to the urban and democratic ideals of a "mobocracy"? Why do we have a generation gap, a revolution of rising expectations, a new unreason, a decline of religion, a changing popular culture? And, if these sources of social conflict have indeed come to pass, and to plague us, who is responsible?

All of these questions are answered by Kristol with one recurrent phrase: the "new class." And what is this "new class"? Unfortunately, one cannot always be sure just what is is. It is not a C. Wright Millsian "power elite," for it does not—yet—have hegemony over all political affairs and actors of importance. It is still jousting with the business community and perhaps with others for power and leadership positions in society. It is certainly urban, both in values and physical locale. And it is broad in membership and influence. The "new class" pops up so often in Kristol's urban vision, and in his writings generally, that it has almost become a synonym for "evil"; it covers a host of sins.

The "new class" does not belong exclusively to Kristol's lexical domain. It is a term that many neoconservatives use, and they use it in abrasive, negative, and condemning tones. With some of these writers, the term seems to be interchangeable with "intellectuals," "McGovernites," the "counterculture," or occasionally, the

"New Left," all imprecise terms. But Kristol sticks with the "new class"term to a numbing extreme, even though it is not always possible to know what he means by it.

Kristol himself says that the "new class" is not easily defined, but he tries occasionally to provide us with a description.[67] The group consists of an unspecified proportion of people whose college-obtained skills and vocations are important to a "post-industrial society."[68] It also includes scientists, teachers, educational administrators, city planners, psychologists, social workers, doctors and lawyers working in the public sector, upper-level government bureaucrats, the staffs of the larger foundations (although some of these are staffed with a great many neoconservatives; could they be "new class," too?).[69] Perhaps the most important segments of all, are the journalists and others in the communications industries. The "new class" is comprised of a large proportion of people who work with words for a living. This fairly populous "new class," in Kristol's view, is indispensable to the functioning of our present-day, urbanized, technological society, and it is disproportionately powerful. Kristol stresses the point that "it is also an ambitious and frustrated class."[70]

The "new class" is antidemocratic and elitist, even though it considers itself a force for social equality.[71] Yet its rhetoric is democratic, helping to contribute to the "mob" nature of our urban civilization. And despite its many skills and its strategic placement in the bureaucracies, academia, the media, and other institutions, the group is not necessarily competent. The "new class" is often inept since it is a natural outgrowth of mass education. Members are elitists, but they may not be elite. Many think of themselves as intellectuals, but are called so only as a courtesy.[72] The "new class" mentality, then, is a combination of arrogant unreason and certified, but questionable, expertise. The "people" of this country are more discerning than the "new class," and they are certainly more reasonable.[73]

It can be seen that this well-placed "class" poses great dangers. They have already given us an urban civilization with a culture lacking in civic virtue or in any sense of social or political obligation. But they remain deeply resentful and full of grievances as they seek radical, unspecified change in America. They are not

socialists, thank goodness, says Kristol.[74] Also, they are not
bureaucratic empire-builders. If only they were!, exclaims Kristol,
for he would be more content to see them working for the Environmental Protection Agency or the Occupational Safety and
Health Administration "in pursuit of financial security, status, and
easy routine work."[75] In fact, the "new class" is not at all
bureacratic in its mentality, but is afflicted with a very un-
bureaucratic crusading zeal.

"New class" members, or so it would seem, are not careerists.
They are not dedicated to themselves so much as they are to the
class's causes. Or are they? Kristol must feel there is some hope in
dealing with at least some of the membership, for he urges the
necessity of making room for them. After all, they are not going to
just go away.[76] Moreover, he believes every effort should be
made to co-opt them into the system. He believes this is possible,
and on this he speaks from experience.

In the meantime, the "new class" carries out relentless warfare against its perceived enemy, the American business community,
which it envies and which it wishes to displace. The "new class"
promotes consumerist and environmental causes, agitates for regulation, and demands economic planning, all of which will give
governmental bureaucracies the power to grow and to coerce. The
ultimate threat is that we shall fall, willy-nilly, into a system of state
capitalism.[77] Behind the mockeries of capitalism, which has actually served the "new class" rather well, and behind its odes to equality for the "people" lurks a strong lust for political power.[78] The
"new class" is a rude and crude army of malcontents, and there
seems to be no stopping them. They have already wrought great
havoc, and they have depressed Irving Kristol.

The "new class" and its role in American society, not to mention
the threat that it has become, sounds like a simple fairy tale. The
villain role goes to the "new class," and the heroic roles are for the
"people," the neoconservatives who have sounded the alarm, and
most of all, the stalwarts of the American business community.

In terms of social science analysis, the "new class" is too amorphous to become a meaningful or useful category for study. There
are different definitions given to the "new class" at different times.
Neoconservative writers do not agree on what the "new class" is,
and a vast array of descriptions are used. For example, Barry Bruce-

Briggs, a *Public Interest* contributor, says that the "new class" is a collection of bureaucrats, academics, and media people, and that one of the chief joys of this group is to contemplate the end of the common use of the automobile by the "people."[79] Kristol recently redefined the "new class" in one of his *Wall Street Journal* columns: "To put it crudely: If you think 'New Class,' you are 'New Class'—even if you temporarily work for General Electric or General Motors, or even if you are still a college freshman. . . ."[80] The "new class" is a set of people who think in a certain way—elitist, anticapitalist, antidemocratic, pro-regulation. The "new class" is "class conscious."[81] But describing a class of people who think in a certain way, especially in the definition supplied by Kristol, gives us no understanding of urban America, its problems, or the political system. It is a convenient thumping-board for Kristol, and little else. Were we to accept the preceding parts of Kristol's analysis—the need for republican government in the face of today's urban civilization, the paralysis due to the intractability of urban problems, the philosophical acceptance of urban decline, and the development of a mass "mob" psychology—it would still be difficult to find the "new class" very helpful as an explanation or as a device used for the purposes of explanation.

Urban life and its discontents are more complex than this particular urban vision. More appears to be awry than the mere emergence of a "new class." And if indeed we are an urban civilization, that could be a reason for hope.

Kristol's Urban Policies, Suggestions, and Scapegoating

Irving Kristol's writings exhibit a predilection for broad, encompassing themes. The themes become all too familiar—the defense of capitalism, the civic virtue of the American people (or its lack), or the latest outrages of the "new class"—but these are the stuff to which he likes to commit mind and spleen. His policy recommendations are sometimes no more than vague suggestions. Occasionally, they are lost altogether in the pursuit of constructing an appropriate and correct set of attitudes that society and government should uphold.

Nevertheless, policy prescriptions for Kristol's City of the Right can be found, although a few of them are not too helpful because they are mentioned only in passing. Kristol does not like school lunch programs, for example, but we cannot be sure why. At other times, his gift for hyperbole takes over and his policy views are only a byproduct: "In the United States today, the law insists that an 18 year-old girl has the right to public fornication in a pornographic movie—but only if she is paid the minimum wage."[82]

A further difficulty in ascertaining Kristol's policies is his tendency to regard many issues (poverty, for example, or the resuscitation of our Northeastern cities) as *nonissues*. He feels that these are issues only because the "new class" has invented them, because college students do not always have good sense when making demands, or because the American underclass has not proved to be smart in the way it handles money. Politicians and the media are greatly at fault in the game of making issues out of whole cloth. They pose impossible ideals they know the nation cannot fulfill, just as Banfield says they do, and the result is frustration and disillusionment in our cities.[83]

Not all of Kristol's prescriptions are policies *per se*, but instead they are approaches to policies that he feels are pragmatic from a political standpoint. In other words, they are statements of political advice on how best to handle certain policies. Two essays, for example, are devoted to the Republican Party's need to win the presidency and still remain popular. The party's perennial difficulty, he finds, is that its sense of fiscal responsibility, imposed after years of Democratic free-spending and boondoggling, gives the GOP the image of dour austerity. And after a few years of straightening out the mess, the Republicans are rewarded with the loss of power because no one wants to quit celebrating and partying on a permanent basis. Then, of course, money flows like water again until the party of Lincoln comes back to turn off the tap. To avoid being trapped in this morass, Kristol advises, the Republicans should spend freely on defense, cut taxes to enhance their popularity and inhibit Democratic spending when that party returns to power, giving the budget deficit no more than secondary consideration. Naturally, he does not recommend anything as mistaken as spending more money on the cities.[84] This may be wise counsel, but its premises are rather far-fetched. Republican presidents Eisenhower, Nixon, and Ford all set new precedents as budget-busters, and Reagan appears likely to do the same.

Kristol's political advice to the Republicans includes an appeal that they accept the premises of the welfare state. Economic and political reality, as well as the hope for long-range success of their party, requires this.[85] Grudging acceptance of a minimally protective welfare state is, after all, one of the distinguishing hallmarks of Kristol and the neoconservatives, and their startling success of the past few years should perhaps be appreciated as an example. Many existing welfare-state measures, however, are considered ripe for repeal. The programs aimed at alleviating (or abolishing) poverty, most of them instituted under Johnson's presidency, are regarded as foolish in conception and irrational and even destructive in practice. Poverty can be eliminated only through economic growth, Kristol maintains. Any other attempt is doomed because no amount of feasible income redistribution could do the job.[86] Poverty, in any event, cannot be eliminated because it is continually redefined to an ever-higher "poverty line." Poverty is also "more than a simple shortage of money. Poverty . . . is defined to a substantial degree by the way in which one copes with poverty."[87]

Kristol further believes that workable welfare programs are those that do not seek to define poverty, but which make all persons eligible for their benefits. Social Security, national health insurance, and family allowance payments are good examples.[88] They also do not breed social conflicts; and they do not polarize. They do not emphasize equality, an unattainable as well as undesirable goal.

Taxation, an issue generally skirted by Kristol, is resented, he says, because of "Great Society" welfare-state measures. But the problem of tax inequity is of no great concern to the people, he asserts. Their resentment is directed against *"taxes, period."*[89] Middle-class Americans simply do not like bleeding hearts and do-gooders to figure out ways society may benefit at their expense: as Kristol sees it, "In the Judeo-Christian tradition, an idealist was someone who, in a spirit of charity, gave away his own money to those less fortunate than he. Today an idealist is someone who, in a spirit of compassion, gives away other people's money."[90] This kind of statement sheds more heat than light on the issue, but

Kristol is correct when he says that there is widspread resentment against any number of welfare state measures.[91] He may be incorrect, however, in saying that people do not care about tax burdens being unfairly allocated.

Most people would probably agree with Kristol when he says that many welfare programs have devastating effects on families and that this is a principal impetus for reform. In one of Kristol's most careless articles, however, he makes the quite tragic mistake of repeating Moynihan's hasty conclusion that disintegration of black families in the cities has led to a ballooning of welfare rolls. No evidence exists for this, according to Frances Fox Piven and Richard A. Cloward in a well-documented book quoted by Kristol in the same article.[92] Kristol's eagerness to score debate points can lead him into misquoting the evidence located right under his nose.

In race relations, an area of absolutely crucial importance to the cities, Kristol's writings offer relatively little. Naturally, he is concerned, but, unfortunately, his only major contribution is a 1965 article with the awful title of "A Few Kind Words for Uncle Tom." This piece is critical of militant blacks who are seen as far too harsh on middle-class blacks just beginning to enjoy the benefits that, until recently, almost no blacks enjoyed. Should their harsh attitude continue, it will work against black attempts to achieve self-identity and group identity.[93] This somewhat cloudy view of the black minority in the cities and in America generally does not appear to be very insightful. Kristol, in fact, seldom broaches the topics of race relations or civil rights. His approaches to those issues that concern urban blacks the most—redevelopment, housing, jobs, education, social services, and income distribution—are usually more general in nature. Indeed, Kristol seems rather unaware of the specific problems confronting blacks today. More apparent is his lack of sympathy for anything other than a neoconservative position on these issues that probably puts him beyond the pale as far as blacks are concerned. A few black leaders and intellectuals (Thomas Sowell comes to mind) might disagree with this assessment and find that Kristol's policies actually do more for blacks, but most would not.

Kristol's views on education, for example, fit the extreme conservative mold rather well. Like the other four thinkers who are shaping the City of the Right, Kristol hates and denigrates our system of free public education. He admits that press sensationalism and other factors have created a "social hypochondria" inflating the problems of the public schools.[94] This is not enough of a mitigating factor, however, to prevent his advocating the familiar conservative cry for voucher systems.[95] The voucher system is strongly supported by all five of the City of the Right protagonists discussed here. Before a voucher system was established, Kristol would not worry much about educational expenditures; he might even like to see them cut quite severely. It does not matter, he says, whether students are educated in old or new buildings, whether they have a library in their school, or whether they have a nice gymnasium or lunchroom. (Remember, Kristol does not care for school-lunch programs in any event.) Pupil-teacher ratios are likewise unimportant from an academic standpoint: "Students who do well in small classes will do well in large ones." Academic achievement is seen as a matter of genetic endowment supplemented by the rearing received at home. At the same time, we are asking too much of our schools, says Kristol, by requiring them to take on all of the social problems caused by poorly motivated students. School expectations have been hopelessly utopian.[96] Like Banfield and Buckley, Kristol supports class-based education and obviously dislikes the mixing of well-motivated, probably middle-class students with the rabble.

Kristol nevertheless seems positively passive about the public schools when compared to what he believes about universities today. He considers higher education a disaster area that hardly deserves to be referred to as anything "higher." Indeed, "a significant minority of today's student body obviously consists of a mob. . . ."[97] Urban civilization and its "mob" characteristics have obviously reached deeply into campus life, so that colleges and universities have long given up the thought of educating students, preferring, whenever possible, to just avoid trouble. According to Kristol, "Quite a few of our universities have already decided that the only way to avoid on-campus riots is to give students academic credit for off-campus rioting ('field work' in the ghettos, among migrant workers, etc.)[98]

Kristol has a cynical view of every aspect of higher education—professors, curriculum, administrators, students, and the institution of faculty tenure. Not all of his criticisms are shrill or invalid. Many of the complaints he registers about academic administrators not knowing what to do and therefore simply copying one another can undoubtedly touch a nerve. His belief that tenure probably sets up sinecures for the incompetent more than it protects the civil liberties of anyone is difficult to dispute. But at times Kristol is contradictory. He states that sociology is a discipline failing to challenge the minds of its students—their passions are "never disturbed by a sociological idea." But let their passions get stirred by sociological ideas *outside* the classroom and they are out of Kristol's good graces.

As for the financing of higher education, Kristol comes up with a voucher system, one which would cross state lines and would permit students to mitigate the effects of out-of-state fees. This might be very helpful to Sun-Belt universities, but it might hurt cold-climate state universities such as Minnesota or Wisconsin. One of Kristol's most callous suggestions is that the financing of higher education should be carried out through a system of student (and perhaps parent) loans rather than through taxation.[99] Not only would such a financing system fall as an unequal burden upon various people and endanger equality of opportunity for a university education, but it would stand in stark contrast to Kristol's CCNY education: a free, no-tuition, tax-supported four years. How can Irving Kristol forget this fact in his own background? How could we be assured, for example, that we would have the benefit of his writings and lectures today had he not been given this chance? Unfortunately, City College and the City University of New York system no longer have tuition-free financing, so opportunities are already less equal than they once were on that important score. Kristol's policy position says a lot about the evolution of his outlook and the elitism it has produced over the years.

The years have also marked a profound change in Kristol's positions on labor unions. It is true that on a personal level he has seemed to enjoy cordial relationships with some labor leaders, particularly those from the cold war arm of the labor movement. It is also true that Kristol, who has a lot of good things to say about American business, cannot say very much that is positive about labor. He believes, for example, that public employees' unions should never go on strike, and the fact that they do is another manifestation of our mobbish urban civilization.[100] He is against the minimum wage, one of labor's principal demands.[101] He has no sympathy for the workers whose lives are disrupted and even ruined by the "regional shift" now occurring as industry flees from the Northeast and Midwest to the Sun Belt. He asks rhetorically, "But where will these poor people go? Well, since this is a free country, they will go where they wish to go—presumably where the jobs are."[102] The American worker is able enough to pull up stakes, to break ties with community and perhaps family and friends for the sake of accommodating the wanderlust of industry. The worker can give up his or her neighborhood, associations, and perhaps the pension that had been counted upon; certainly workers ought to give up their unions in exchange for the anti-union hostility of the South and Southwest.

Kristol's brusque approach to labor relations is equaled by his cost-efficient approach to urban development issues: cost-efficient, that is, in traditional economic terms, but not necessarily in terms of aesthetic, land-optimizing, environmental, or community considerations. It is only a slight exaggeration to say that Kristol is pro-development and anti-environment.[103] He tends to believe in development for its own sake, though he takes aim at city planners from time to time for letting old buildings face the wrecker's ball prematurely.[104] He dislikes urban renewal schemes, as most conservatives do; though this is not completely clear, it appears that his major objection to them is that they are government-controlled. If urban renewal were to be carried out by private developers, it would probably meet with Kristol's indifference or even approval.

The environmental cause, which Kristol terms "eco-mania," is condemned as a malignant blot on our cities. He says that environmentalists have not even had the decency to stay within the bounds of the Judeo-Christian ethic. They are pagans in fact and in deed. Yet they are an important part of our urban civilization, to be sure, because they reach beyond reason in order to blast our technology and the capitalist sytem linked to it. In Kristol's mind it is true, of course, that at some future time our planet and its sun will be dead, but "the idea that we must all live now so as to delay that eventuality by perhaps a couple of hundred years is obviously preposterous.'' We may not have religious instruction in our public schools anymore, he continues, but a lot of it takes place, anyway, because of this neopaganism.[105] The environmental movement and its bureaucratic supporters constitute nothing less than fanaticism. They urge high-density housing projects and an end to suburban sprawl because of aesthetic objections to the automobile. They express concern about noise pollution in the ghetto, when we know that noise is a part of life there. Kristol views environmentalism as an invention of the ''new class'' that fits well with its rejection of economic sense and its insistence upon governing the preferences of the people, who know their wants and desires without being told what they should be.[106] (On this particular issue, though certainly not on others, the people possess bourgeois civic virtue.)

Kristol knows what is good for the people, however, when it comes to the issue of censorship. He favors it. To assert that certain books or movies cannot degrade humanity is logically to reject the possibility that we can be uplifted by the worthwhile and the wholesome.[107] Kristol takes a rather more reactionary view on this policy question than some of the other City of the Right thinkers, notably Milton Friedman and Ayn Rand.

Libertarianism, as we have seen, is not Kristol's strong suit. His indulgent position on the issue of McCarthyism, his inept (if not evasive) handling of *Encounter's* ties with the CIA, his insistence upon corporate free movement to accommodate the regional shift to the Sun Belt while shrugging off workers' rights of movement, and his indifference to equal protection and equality of opportunity add up to a painfully obvious ranking of priorities. And his antidemocracy stance that is the subject of so many of Kristol's essays often strays beyond a repudiation of popular government merely because of the preferred virtues of bourgeois republicanism. The vitriol extends to life styles and value preferences, choices that may have little to do with politics or society. Kristol's concerns and the bitterness which expresses them should give any libertarian pause.

In support of Kristol it must be conceded that no thoughtful observer of urban America today can be without qualms. Some of the currents he describes and decries—narcissism, hedonism, unfocused rage and alienation—are clearly in existence. The important point is, how does one interpret these trends and their context? Might capitalism, for example, be a cause of this alienation? In some passages of his essays, Kristol seems to hint at this possibility. Has the counterculture given us a retrograde set of values? Or is it pointing in new directions which may reform, renourish, and rebuild our cities? Will censorship help reestablish the civic virtue that Kristol finds lacking in our urban civilization—or will it lead to a greater conformity? Is equality of opportunity in education passé because Kristol and many of the prominent neoconservatives managed to get their free education at CCNY long ago?

A detailed search through Kristol's vision of the city, through his policy positions, through the panoply of his neoconservatism demonstrate, finally, that neoconservatism is neither so new nor fresh in its approach as one might hope. Some provocative points are made, some parries and thrusts occur, but in the end, a terrible pessimism hangs over neoconservatism. How terrible that blacks make demands, unions call strikes, the poor express their discontent, and a new generation deigns to thumb its nose at such sacred cows as technology, suburbia, tax privilege, and corporations! A "new class," possessed by an inverted sense of values, seeks status, power, and the sheer joy of perversity by sneering at business, middle America, and tradition.

Does such a "new class" exist? Has it indeed helped create a mob-centered urban civilization? Or has Kristol fallen into some misperceptions, some of which are quite fanciful? Yes, it appears he has. His hearkening back to a more virtuous bourgeois society indicates that not all of his utopianism went the way of his Trotskyist views. Kristol has formulated an explanation of our urban problems and discontents that is probably more elaborate than necessary. It could be a more thoughtful and productive task, perhaps, to listen to the grievances emerging from our contemporary urban experience and to examine them in the light of more direct and objective criteria and evidence than that of a "new class" and its shadowy existence or of a citizenry that fails to measure up to a preconceived notion of collective virtue. Some of the grievances, we can be sure, are real; and some of the attempts to aright them are sincere. Let us start with that knowledge, and—who knows?—we may find ourselves attacking problems rather than each other. At present, unfortunately, Irving Kristol and his neoconservatism are given to odd, unproductive and, at times, vituperative scapegoating and reasoning processes having little to do with civic virtue of any kind.

Notes

1. Joseph Epstein, "The New Conservatives: Intellectuals in Retreat," in *The New Conservatives: A Critique from the Left*, ed. by Lewis A. Coser and Irving Howe (New York: New American Library, 1976), p. 13.

2. Peter Steinfels, *The Neoconservatives* (New York: Simon and Schuster, 1979), p. 81; Irving Kristol, *Two Cheers for Capitalism* (New York: Basic Books, 1978), p. xiv.

3. In politics, says Kristol, "ideas are all-important"; *Two Cheers for Capitalism,* p. 158. In *The Neoconservatives,* Stenfels notes that the Marxist-Leninist backgound of a number of neoconservatives sheds light upon their belief in the role of intellectuals as the vanguard of the not-very-discerning-but-noble masses; p. 285. This view, however, seems to imply that both radicals and neoconservatives hold the "masses" in contempt and to an equivalent degree.

4. Peter Steinfels, *The Neoconservatives*, chapter 5.

5. Irving Howe, "The New York Intellectuals," *Commentary* 47 (January 1969): 14-16.

6. Irving Kristol, "The New York Intellectuals," *Commentary* 47 (January 1969): p. 12.

7. Nathan Glazer, "Kristol and the New York Intellectual Establishment," *Alternative* (now *American Spectator*) 5 (June-September 1972): pp. 6-7.

8. Kristol, *Two Cheers for Capitalism*, p. 59.

9. Glazer, "Kristol and the New York Intellectual Establishment," pp. 6-7.

10. Some examples: *Two Cheers for Capitalism*; Irving Kristol, *On the Democratic Idea in America* (New York: Harper and Row, 1972), chapters 2 and 6; Irving Kristol, "Capitalism, Socialism and Democracy," *Commentary* 65 (April 1978) pp. 53-54; *Wall Street Journal*, June 26, 1979.

11. Quoted in Peter Steinfels, *The Neoconservatives*, p. 82.

12. Kristol, "The New York Intellectuals," p.14.

13. Howe, "The New York Intellectuals," p. 16.

14. Peter Steinfels, *The Neoconservatives*, p. 87. A "Weekend Competition" entry by Gavin Ewart in *New Statesman* 101 (January 2, 1981), p. 25, succinctly describes *Encounter*.

15. Quoted in Steinfels, *The Neoconservatives*, p. 89.

16. Ibid., p. 52.

17. This is Steinfels's definition; *The Neoconservatives*, pp. 4-7.

18. Descriptions of the various activities of the neoconservatives are set out in Steinfels, *Neoconservatives,* especially pp. 4-9.

19. Robert Bartley, "Irving Kristol and the Public Interest Crowd," *Alternative* 5 (June-September 1972): p. 5.

20. Irving Kristol, "Foreign Policy and the American Jewish Community," *ADL* (Anti-Defamation League) *Bulletin*, September 1980, p. 1.

21. Kristol, *Two Cheers for Capitalism*, p. 127-28.

22. Ibid.

23. Ibid., p. 121.

24. "Kristol has come 'to believe that an adult's "normal" political instincts should be' conservative. Not to be is at best 'immature,' at worst 'abnormal,' " says Steinfels, *Neoconservatives*, p. 23.

25. Ibid., p. 104.

26. Steinfels, *Neoconservatives*, quoted in review by Peter H. Schuck, *Wall Street Journal*, July 3, 1979.

27. Steinfels, *Neoconservatives,* p. 106.

28. Ibid., p. 42.

29. Ibid., p. 224; Epstein, "The New Conservatives: Intelectuals in Retreat," p. 28.

30. Bartley, "Irving Kristol and the Public Interest Crowd," p. 6.

31. On the Left, the Caucus for a New Political Science and the Union of Radical Sociologists, to cite just two examples, were founded in the 1960s upon the issue of values in social science.

32. Steinfels, *Neoconservatives*, p. 73; also, see Epstein, "The New Conservatives: Intellectuals in Retreat," pp. 22-23.

33. Kristol quoted in Michael Walzer, "In Defense of Equality," in *The New Conservatives: A Critique from the Left,* pp. 108-9.

34. Kristol, *On the Democratic Idea in America*, p. 124.

35. Irving Kristol, "Socialism: An Obituary for an Idea," *Alternative* 10 (October 1976): 7.

36. Kristol, "Foreign Policy and the American Jewish Community," p. 14.

37. Irving Kristol, "The American Revoluion as a Successful Revolution," in *The American Revolution: Three Views* (New York: American Brands, 1975), pp. 30, 42-44; also published as *America's Continuing Revolution: An Act of Conservation* (Washington: American Enterprise Institute, 1973, 1974, and 1975).

38. Kristol, *On the Democratic Idea in America*, p. 92.

39. Ibid., pp. 98-99.

40. Kristol, *Two Cheers for Capitalism*, p. 59.

41. Irving Kristol, "Republican Virtue vs. Servile Institutions," *Alternative* 8 (February 1975): 6.

42. Kristol, "The American Revolution as a Successful Revolution," p. 43.

43. Kristol, "The American Revolution as a Successful Revolution," p. 43; Kristol, *Two Cheers for Capitalism*, p. ix.

44. Kristol, *Two Cheers for Capitalism*, p. xi.

45. Irving Kristol, "The Adversary Culture of Intellectuals," *Encounter* 53 (October 1979): 14.

46. Kristol, "Republican Virtue vs. Servile Institutions," p. 5.

47. Ibid.

48. Kristol quoted in R. Emmett Tyrrell, review of *On the Democratic Idea in America, Alternative* 5 (June-September 1972): 9.

49. Quoted by Steinfels, *Neoconservatives,* p. 92.

50. Kristol, *Two Cheers for Capitalism*, p. 237.

51. Kristol, *On the Democratic Idea in America,* p. 101

52. Irving Kristol, "Blame It on the People!" *Wall Street Journal,* July 19, 1979; also see Steinfels, *Neoconservatives,* pp. 102-3, 248, 260.

53. Kristol, *On the Democratic Idea in America*, chapter one, "Urban Civilization and Its Discontents," especially p. 17.

54. Kristol, *On the Democratic Idea in America,* p. 101.

55. Kristol, *On the Democratic Idea in America,* p. 7.

56. Irving Kristol, "An Urban Civilization Without Cities?" *Horizon* 14 (Autumn 1972): 36-37.

57. Irving Kristol, "Sense and Nonsense in Urban Policy," *Nation's Cities* 16 (February 1978): 23.

58. Kristol, *On the Democratic Idea in America,* p. 9.

59. Kristol, "An Urban Civilization Without Cities?" pp. 39-41; "Sense and Nonsense in Urban Policy," p. 24.

60. Kristol, *On the Democratic Idea in America,* p. 21.

61. Kristol, *On the Democratic Idea in America,* pp. 4-6.

62. "It is the startling absence of values that represents the authentic 'urban crisis' of our democratic, urban nations"; Kristol, *On the Democratic Idea in America*, p. 20.

63. Kristol, *On the Democratic Idea in America,* pp. 15-21; "An Urban Civilization Without Cities?" pp. 38-40.

64. Kristol, *On the Democratic Idea in America,* pp. 25-29.

65. Ibid., p. 28.

66. Kristol, "An Urban Civilization Without Cities?" p. 37.

67. Kristol defines the "new class" in two different essays in *Two Cheers for Capitalism*, pp. 14, 25; see also Kristol, "The 'New Class' Revisited," *Wall Street Journal*, May 31, 1979.

68. Kristol, *Two Cheers for Capitalism*, p. 25.

69. "Now and then a neoconservative like Kristol will own up to membership in the 'new class,' " according to Steinfels, *Neoconservatives*, p. 286. It is hardly surprising, considering the breadth of this category of people.

70. Kristol, *Two Cheers for Capitalism*, p. 25.

71. Ibid., p. 162.

72. Kristol, *On the Democratic Idea in America*, pp. 85-86.

73. Kristol, *Two Cheers for Capitalism*, p. 164.

74. Quoted in Steinfels, *Neoconservatives*, p. 261.

75. Kristol, "The 'New Class' Revisited," *Wall Street Journal*, May 31, 1979.

76. Quoted in Peter Steinfels, *Neoconservatives*, p. 260.

77. Kristol, *Two Cheers for Capitalism*, p. 20.

78. Kristol, "The 'New Class' Revisited," *Wall Street Journal,* May 31, 1979.

79. Barry Bruce-Briggs, *The War Against the Automobile* (New York: E. P. Dutton, 1977).

80. Kristol, "The 'New Class' Revisited," *Wall Street Journal,* May 31, 1979.

81. Ibid.

82. Quoted in Steinfels, *Neoconservatives,* p. 96.

83. Kristol, *On the Democratic Idea in America*, p. 141.

84. Kristol, *Two Cheers for Capitalism*, pp. 117, 120, 124; Irving Kristol, "The Battle for Reagan's Soul," *Wall Street Journal*, May 16, 1980.

85. Kristol, *Two Cheers for Capitalism*, pp. 118-119.

86. Kristol, *On the Democratic Idea in America*, p. 140.

87. Kristol, *Two Cheers for Capitalism,* pp. 219, 220, 225.

88. Ibid., pp. 231-232.

89. Ibid., p. 212.

90. Quoted in Steinfels, *Neoconservatives*, p. 96.

91. In the wake of California's tax-cutting Proposition 13, passed in a 1978 referendum, several opinion polls in that state and in the nation at large asked what is the best area in which to cut budgets. In most cases, "welfare" was the first item listed by respondents.

92. Irving Kristol, "Welfare: The Best of Intentions, the Worst of

Results," *Atlantic Monthly* 228 (August 1971): 45-47; Frances Fox Piven and Richard A. Cloward, *Regulating the Poor: The Functions of Public Welfare* (New York: Random House Vintage Books, 1971), pp. 192-96.

93. Irving Kristol, "A Few Kind Words for Uncle Tom," *Harpers*, 230 (February 1965): 95-99.

94. Joseph Epstein, "The New Conservatives: Intellectuals in Retreat," p. 25.

95. Kristol, *On the Democratic Idea in America,* pp. 121-22; this particular passage deals with universities, but it is reasonable to infer from it that he also applies this policy goal to the public schools.

96. Kristol, *On the Democratic Idea in America*, p. 145-48.

97. Kristol, *On the Democratic Idea in America,* p. 115.

98. Ibid., p. 124.

99. Kristol, *On the Democratic Idea in America,* p. 117-22.

100. Kristol, "Republican Virtue vs. Servile Institutions," p. 8.

101. Quoted in Steinfels, *Neoconservatives,* p. 96.

102. Kristol, "Sense and Nonsense in Urban Policy," p. 24.

103. Kristol, *Two Cheers for Capitalism*, p. 145.

104. Kristol, *Two Cheers for Capitalism*, pp. 40-43, 57; Kristol, "Of Economics and 'Eco-Mania,' " *Wall Street Journal*, September 19, 1970.

105. Kristol, *Two Cheers for Capitalism*, p. 57.

106. Kristol, *On the Democratic Idea in America,* chapter 3, "Pornography, Obscenity, and the Case for Censorship."

107. Kristol, "Of Economics and 'Eco-Mania.' "

6

AYN RAND:

SKYSCRAPER ROMANCE

*If there is a novelist with universal appeal among
the Reagan organization, it is Ayn Rand, proponent
of enlightened self-interest. Some of Reagan's
close advisers, including his director of domestic
policy, Martin Anderson, sat at her feet when they
were fledgling disciples and a Reagan Presidency
just a gleam in the eye of G. E. Theater's host.* [1]

Most social scientists have had a chance to become acquainted,
at one time or another, with the Objectivist ideology of Ayn Rand
and her followers. The tendency is to airily dismiss her. It is known,
after all, that Ayn Rand is some kind of right-wing extremist,
that she espouses an incomplete and often inconsistent set of principles, and that much of her philosophy must be ferreted out of her
long (and often boring) works of fiction, such as *Atlas Shrugged*
and *The Fountainhead*. Many of these same social scientists,
however, have had the more than occasional experience of a student, usually an undergraduate, walking up to the lectern at the end
of class and asking, starry-eyed, "Have you ever read any of the
works of Ayn Rand?" Whether intellectuals ignore her has not proved to be a very important consideration, for Ayn Rand has a large

and dedicated following. Millions of copies of her books have been sold, and they continue to sell in the range of more than 100,000 per year.[2] Her radio and television appearances, her *Objectivist Newsletter,* her interviews in such wide-circulation magazines as *Playboy,* and most of all, her cult following, make her a formidable figure in the world of political thought and controversy.[3] She is also the architect (a term that would please her) of a distinctive view of urban life, one which celebrates urban places and values and denigrates nature and country life while it simultaneously glorifies capitalism, industry, technology, individualism, creativity, and laissez-faire economics.

Like Buckley, Rand is a conservative with an appeal potent enough to claim thousands, if not millions, of adherents. She is therefore a most fitting subject for a study of conservative visions of the city. As a conservative she is unique; not all of the terms of reference of conservatism in American life today can be applied to her. Moreover, her urban vision is but one component, though in many ways the most important, of her philosophy. She does have a world view of political issues, and this is largely defined by the great clashes she sees taking place: individualism versus collectivism, the subjgation of nature in order to fulfill the purposes of humankind, and "the role of mind in man's existence."[4] Rand's urban vision, then, is greatly affected by her world view, and urban issues are often microcosmic counterparts of much broader and more earthshaking considerations.

Rand is not classified invariably as a conservative; indeed, much about her outlook and values seems to defy classification.[5] She has openly demonstrated her disdain for the John Birch Society and for such conservative heroes as the late Senator Joseph McCarthy. She supported Barry Goldwater's campaign for president in 1964, but she criticized that cause for failing to be an intellectual effort. She believes that a great deal of what passes for conservatism in American politics is simply a superficial, inconsistent, intellectually barren attachment to the past.[6] As its common denominator, it often exhibits "a folksy, 'cracker-barrel,' mass oriented kind of anti-intellectual reliance on faith ('the heart') and on 'tradition.' "[7] She takes conservatives to task for their gross lack of libertarian sensitivity and for their racism:

If one wishes to gauge the relationship of freedom to the goals of today's intellectuals, one may gauge it by the fact that the concept of individual rights is evaded, distorted, perverted and seldom discussed, most conspicuously seldom by the so-called "conservatives."[8]

One of the worst contradictions . . . is the stand of many so-called "conservatives" . . . who claim to be defenders of freedom, of capitalism, of property rights, of the Constitution, yet who advocate racism at the same time . . . they are cutting the ground from under their own feet. Men who deny individual rights cannot claim, defend or uphold any rights whatsoever. It is such alleged champions of capitalism who are helping to discredit and destroy it.[9]

Many of Rand's followers share concerns with the political Left in America and have even found common ground on a host of issues: the war in Vietnam, the draft, the American state-corporate economic nexus, laws regulating abortions and various sexual practices, curtailment of civil liberties, and local control of civic institutions.[10] Both groups have, in addition, opposed censorship of films and books. Where the two groups part company is in the area of economic theory, especially as it pertains to property rights.

Rand disapproves of many conservatives whom she considers ineffective as champions of capitalism and individualism. She believes that their lack of libertarian sensibility and their racism are bad enough, both in principle and in setting an example for the capitalist cause, but the acts and words of conservatives also demonstrate their ineptitude. This ineptitude has led to dreadful compromises with liberal and socialist statism. Conservative politicians, she notes, like to talk about a "mixed economy" and have helped to establish many laws that interfere with free-market capitalism—anti-trust laws, minimum wages, public housing, government aid to industries and various interest groups, and various welfare state measures.[11] Her most caustic criticism of conservatives, however, is reserved for the mystics whose moral code is tied to religion. In conceding the realm of reason to the statists and to the Left, she asserts, conservatives choose to abandon their most powerful intellectual weapon. Reason, Rand argues, is, after all, on the side of capitalism and of conservatives generally, and to rest one's case on faith is to substitute religion, a purely private matter, for the rational basis of capitalism, which the public needs to understand. Rand is so deeply individualistic that she cannot bring herself to believe in a higher life form than human beings; she therefore sees only futility in the habit of many conservatives of finding a religious basis for capitalism.[12]

Is Rand a conservative? Most definitely. She opposes all welfare state measures, she dislikes labor unions, she steadfastly supports capitalism and hates socialism. She believes in unfettered corporate privilege, she opposes all consumer and environmental legislation, and she upholds private property and the "free market" as the major institutions that protect our liberties. She endorses the status quo *if* it is not presently possible to move towards her vision of the good society. She opposes all civil rights legislation or any legislation designed to protect minorities. Finally, she supports inequality with a fierceness that puts Buckley or Friedman to shame; indeed, she proclaims morality to be closely tied to— and even measured by—the prices set in the market place and by the "success" one enjoys according to the standards, mostly the financial rewards, of the capitalist system. Her Objectivist philosophy, with its hatred of altruism and its glorification of selfishness, is profoundly conservative in its implications, and it rests ultimately upon an understanding of the garrison function—the Hobbesian function of security provided for the protection of unequal privilege—as the preeminent and most legitimate function of the state.

Rand's philosophy may not be the most traditional form of conservatism. Indeed, tradition does not merit the exalted place in the firmament it is given by other conservatives. Rand is more of an iconoclast than a traditionalist. Objectivism, all the same, is a conservative philosophy, and her urban policy proposals will be shown to be conservative in specific or implied ways.

Ayn Rand was born in St. Petersburg (now Leningrad), Russia, in 1905. She emigrated to the United States in 1926 and became a citizen in 1931. The Russian Revolution was, needless to say, a traumatic experience for her. At the age of twelve, the year of the Revolution, she "first heard the Communist principle that Man should exist for the sake of the State" and decided "that this principle was evil, and that it could lead to nothing but evil. . . ."[13] Her novel, *We the Living*, is somewhat autobiographical.[14] Like Kira, the heroine of the story, Ayn Rand felt stifled and oppressed by Communist doctrine and the new Soviet state. She found some solace there in attending operettas originally produced in the West; these contrasted with the drab conformity of her existence. Her real joy, however, occurred with the arrival of American movies in the early 1920s. Once in a while, she would catch a glimpse of New York City in one of these films. The long slender skyscrapers touched her imagination and gave her a strange kind of hope for the future. Kira has the same experience in *We the Living*.[15] This feeling was possibly the beginning of Rand's urban vision.

She received her university degree in 1924, and arrived in New York two years later with fifty dollars in her pocket. She spent two days just touring the city admiring its neon and steel; the City was "her symbol of everything she admired in life."[16] She wanted to write; in fact, she had wanted to write since the age of nine, and can remember the precise hour and day in which she made this career decision. Since film had become a favorite medium, she was quickly off to Hollywood, where she met producer-director Cecil B. DeMille under the luckiest of circumstances.[17] She felt fortunate to be working with DeMille, and writing consumed most of her life. She had few social contacts, although she did find time to involve herself in the issue of the Communist menace within the film industry. However, Rand never had anything to do with the blacklisting and witchhunting eventually to take over Hollywood in the post-World War II period.[18]

Rand became famous with the publication of *The Fountainhead* in 1943. More than two million copies were sold, and a film was based upon it. The novel is about unbelievable people who play dominance games with one another and spout off incredible statements incessantly in order to make Rand's propaganda points.

The long speeches of *The Fountainhead* are brevity itself, however, compared with the windiness of the characters in *Atlas Shrugged*, which appeared in 1957. Once again, Ayn Rand's novel was in the million-plus copies' bracket. Though more heavy-handed than *The Fountainhead*, *Atlas Shrugged* seems to be the work of which Rand and her followers are most proud.[19] Her other novels have also done well; but few critics would regard any of her works as great literature. Her nonfiction works, comprising a much smaller part of her publications, provide an occasional link between her various premises, assertions, and logical constructs. The development of her urban vision and of the few specific policies she advocates must therefore rely, in the main, upon her works of fiction.

Rand's Objectivism

I know . . . that something which knows how to want
—isn't that life itself?

> —Kira, in *We the Living*.[20]

I swear by my life and my love of it that I will
never live for the sake of another man, nor ask
another man to live for mine.

> —Motto of John Galt,
> hero of *Atlas Shrugged*[21]

Ayn Rand's Objectivism is her original contribution to a conservative view of political life. Objectivism is a point of view—it would be difficult to justify calling it a philosophy—designed within an urban framework. Rand never considers rural residents in her schemes and probably excludes suburbanites also. Places outside the city may be temporary abodes or visiting places for some of her characters, but no more than that. Not even John Galt's valley community in *Atlas Shrugged* can take on a sense of permanence. Objectivism proceeds from urban assumptions and premises, for urbanism is the triumph of creative people over nature.

Objectivism holds that there are objective truths and rules of human conduct that are derived from the use of reason and the terms of self-interest. When these Objectivist precepts are discovered, they can allegedly be built into a set of logically connected constructs. Rationality and self-interest are, for all practical purposes, synonymous in Rand's scheme. They stand in stark opposition to altruism and charity, impulses that are considered the bane of Western civilization.

In many respects objectivism can be considered a war against altruism, a cause that is antithetical to everyone's best interests and, ultimately, is merely used by the proponents of Statism as a means of obtaining power at everyone's expense. Selfishness is the personal and self-evident need of all individuals; as Rand describes it, it is really a virtue that should be encouraged. Property rights and the attendant right of free trade (in other words, a laissez-faire economic system along the lines of the Adam Smith classical model) are central to Objectivism and to the individualism at its core. This individualism, in turn, finds identity and expression through creativity. But creativity seems to take on several special meanings in Rand's world, perhaps most strongly concentrated in just a few fields of endeavor—architecture, art, writing, and, most certainly, entrepreneurship. The captains of industry are perhaps the most creative of all. Whatever the field of work, competence is the key, and the theme of competence threads its way through all of Rand's fiction. It is the competence of the country's great minds, after all, that makes it possible for John Galt to lead a "mind strike" in *Atlas Shrugged*. It is competence that makes Howard Roark of *The Fountainhead* beloved by his employees, even though he is unapproachable, almost inhuman, and never one to engage in small talk:

He responded only to the essence of a man: to his creative capacity. In this office one had to be competent. There were no alternatives, no mitigating situations. But if a man worked well, he needed nothing else to win his employer's benevolence: it was granted, not as a gift, but as a debt. It was granted, not as affection, but as recognition. It bred an immense feeling of self-respect. . . .[22]

No state or society, of course, has ever existed in accordance with
the Objectivist model, but of all the societies the world has known,
the United States has the greatest potential for the adoption
of these values. The United States is a land of "superlative material
achievement in the midst of an untouched wilderness. . . ."[23]
Its only lack, according to Rand, is a coherent philosophy to
defend it and the capitalist ethos it has created. Capitalism is the
economic and political system which affords maximum creativity,
entrepreneurship and assertion of individualism. It is, in fact, the
unknown ideal, according to one of Rand's titles.

The task of Objectivism, therefore, is to provide capitalism with
an intellectual defense. Why have we had to wait for Ayn Rand and
Objectivism to see such a defense formulated? Because capitalists
have been too busy making money and building America into the
great industrial society it has become! So says industrialist Francisco d'Anconia in *Atlas Shrugged*: "We produced the wealth of
the world—but we let our enemies write its moral code."[24] This
moral code, presumably, is guided by the hateful cause of altruism.
Rand presumes that only the capitalist class can produce wealth,
not workers, mere underlings; she further presumes that somehow
this capitalist class has failed to make an impact upon our institutions of government, law, and policymaking. Just a case of neglect,
no doubt. The Congress, the bureacracy, the independent
regulatory commissions—all of them have been overlooked.

Rand is contemptuous of all modern philosophy as either too
subjective, too trivial, or too conniving.[25] It fails to recognize that
"There are no conflicts of interests among rational men."[26] After
all, rationality and the rules of self-interest are discoverable and
discernible. The truth that there is no such entity as society is
relatively easy to find, since society is only a number—a collec-
tivity—of individuals.[27] Society therefore has no rights. Collec-
tivities do not have rights. Groups have no rights. Rand says that
the notion of collective rights ultimately means that rights belong to
some people, but not to others. Collectivism therefore perverts the
rights of individuals, and, to Rand, it is analogous in the realm of
politics to what subjectivism is in the realm of ethics. Collectivism is
amoral; it replaces the rights of humankind with the rights of the

mob.[28] Howard Roark tells us that there is no such thing as a collective brain.[29] The illegitimacy of collectivism also means that there is no "public interest."[30]

Individual rights are therefore the only rights. They are the means by which society is made subordinate to moral law, which, incidentally, is the great achievement of America. In some ways, at least, America has managed to keep altruism in a subordinate position.

All of these assumptions point clearly to the one policy position acceptable to Ayn Rand on the question of government-sponsored or-imposed altruism: there can be none. No cleaning up of the slums, no Medicare, no welfare, no protection of unions, and no consumer legislation.[31] Most heartily condemned are those well-known accoutrements of the liberal welfare state: the pluralism of interest groups, each seeking their own special favors from government, the tolerance of a mixed (as opposed to "free") economy, the attempts to develop consensual modes of behavior and policy processes, and the pragmatic approach to politics shaping all of these precepts.[32] And Rand also hates those bleeding hearts whose liberal politics and do-good social values lead them into careers of telling the rest of us what to do: social workers, bureaucrats, sociologists, community organizers, and planners. Look at Emma Chalmers in *Atlas Shrugged*, an errant social engineer, health food faddist, and general meddler: she "was an old sociologist who had hung about Washington for years, as other women of her age and type hang about barrooms."[33]

While altruism is a manifest evil, selfishness is a manifest virtue. Altruism is collectivist or other-directed; selfishness, of course, is seen as residing within the individual. The selfishness defined by Rand is certainly a type of the "spirit of grab" associated with acquisitiveness. But it takes on a brash assertiveness in Objectivism. The only competitor ever envied by railroad founder Nat Taggart in *Atlas Shrugged* was one who said, "The public be damned!"[34] There is, at the same time, a nonacquisitive form of selfishness upheld by Rand and best exemplified by Howard Roark when he turns down the chance offered by Weidler to build a great project because it cannot be built *his* way. In this scene, Weidler complains, "It's sheer insanity! I want you. We want your building. You need the commission. Do you have to be so fanatical and selfless about it?" Roark asked incredulously, "What?" "Fanatical and selfless." Roark smiled. "That was the most selfish thing you've ever seen a man do."[35] Selfishness, obviously, consists of more than materialism. It protects the integrity, character and creativity of the individual.

But such selfishness does not eschew acquisition. Property rights and profits are extremely important to Rand's values and to Objectivism. To a great extent, they offer a measure of success, and a rather precise one at that, for profit and material gain are considered products of the mind.[36] Dagny Taggart and Hank Rearden, two of the industrial giants of *Atlas Shrugged*, are publicly proud of their profiteering.[37] Ayn Rand's attitude towards large corporations is certainly interesting even if it is not consistent. On the one hand she holds out a competitive, laissez-faire economy as the model towards which Objectivism seems to aspire; but since she would never permit antitrust laws or corporate regulation of any kind to take place, she is also apparently ready to let corporations get away with whatever they can in monopolistic or oligopolistic sets of circumstances. She adheres adamantly to the line between private corporate power and the power of government and would have no truck with those who argue that this line is easily erasable, that a "power elite" governance pattern does this erasing, and that recognition of the blurring of this line is the first step towards appreciating the way the American system actually works. She also apparently has little interest in the creativity or innovativeness of small businesses; at least she never chooses to write about them. She may believe that the large corporate entities of this country are headed and run by creative and innovative powers. She has somehow learned to appreciate, in ways not well understood by others, such creativity and innovation as Corvair and Pinto automobiles, Firestone tires, and preservatives used in bacon.

Whatever their sins may be, Ayn Rand does seem to believe that the alternative to the power of giant corporations must necessarily be Big Government, which is the last thing she wants. Corporations therefore help to protect and promote our freedom through their roles as alternative sources of economic power and as arbiters of the free market, and the supposed libertarianism of all of this is asserted by Rand when she says that "a free mind and free market are corollaries."[38]

Since capitalism is the system that best ensures the continuation of individual freedom and individual creative instinct, it follows that property rights hold a special place in Rand's set of values. She believes that property rights are not separable from other human rights, though she also makes the point that they must hold a preeminent place among these rights. This is because they represent the rewards of mind and creativity and because, like Buckley, she thinks that property can insulate one against the state and provide free choices for its owners which would not otherwise be available to them.

Her favorite form of property is buildings, usually tall buildings:

> The skyline of New York is a monument of a splendor that no pyramids or palaces will ever equal or approach. But America's skyscrapers were not built by public funds nor for a public purpose; they were built by the energy, initiative and wealth of private individuals for personal profit.[39]

She loves skyscrapers for their own sake; they are the ultimate aesthetic vision, one nature could never match. But she also loves them for the creativity and acquisitiveness—and selfishness—that they represent. Her books are full of adoring descriptions of these buildings, most particularly the Manhattan skyline. Her heroes and heroines build them, stand on top of them, admire them, think about them, discuss them, and fornicate on their roofs so that they will have the city all around them for inspiration.[40] Central to an understanding of Rand is an appreciation of her belief that buildings, private or public, reflect the social and political landscape of a country. Public buildings, if they are to exist at all, must have some moral significance. Howard Roark, the architect in *The Fountainhead*, builds a Temple of the Human Spirit.[41] The "austere simplicity of Independence Hall" represents "authentic grandeur."[42] Soviet buildings and monuments, in contrast, are barren and lifeless because they were built upon the bodies of exploited people. (Were not those citadels of capitalists, the skyscrapers of

New York, also built by exploited people?)[43] The statements of
Rand on this question do have a point. She is accurate in depicting
architecture as often symbolic of a society or, perhaps more often,
of a regime. We know of the various monumental follies of dictatorial and totalitarian governments, including those of the Soviet
Union, Hitler's Germany, the Shah in Iran, Sukarno in Indonesia,
and so forth. Bigness is valued in and of itself, and the individual is
dwarfed by such buildings. It is even possible to argue that the construction that has gone on in Washington D.C. in recent
years—look at the FBI's J. Edgar Hoover building, or the HUD
Building, the Forrestal Building, or the Rayburn House Office
Building—tends to coincide with the increasing remoteness and, yes,
repression of government.

Much as she dislikes government, Ayn Rand is not an anarchist.
She believes that government has three proper functions, all of
which are involved with the use of physical force: the police power,
so that criminal laws may be enforced; the defense function, to provide against foreign invaders; and the law courts to protect the
rights of people with an objective code of rules. The protection of
elites who have acquired more property than most of us is considered proper and necessary; conversely, governmental protection
of the poor, the weak, the sick, the elderly, the handicapped—in
other words, any social welfare function as the term is generally
understood—should not be tolerated. No income transfers are to
take place, and charity, though she openly discourages it, would be
permitted if people wish to participate in it on a strictly voluntary
basis. Taxation also would be voluntary, although Rand admits
that such a voluntary system would need some time to evolve.[44]

Paradoxically, then, Rand worries about the economic and
political liberties, as she defines them, that are threatened by the
existence of government, but she appears sanguine about state police
power and military power, especially in defense of the causes and
concerns she deems worthwhile. For the poor, the less fortunate,
and the less brainy people of the world, she holds out little practical
hope of bettering their lot. That can only occur, it seems, through
the munificence of inventors, industrialists, and others as a consequence or a by-product of their much-to-be-admired selfishness.

Rand's lack of concern for the poor is rooted in her view of the general public as a great, inert beast.[45] This public sometimes includes the middle class, businessmen, and even the wealthy, but it is the poor who undoubtedly contribute most to this beastiality. Dominique Francon, the romantic heroine in *The Fountainhead*, says that one can feel "some respect for people when they suffer. They have a certain dignity. But have you ever watched them enjoying themselves? That's when you see the truth."[46] Dominique addresses a meeting of militant, radical social workers on the issue of public housing and tells them that if the poor are poor, it is their own fault:

> The family on the first floor . . . do not bother to pay their rent, and the children cannot go to school for lack of clothes. The father has a charge account at a corner speak-easy. He is in good health and has a good job. . . . The couple on the second floor have just purchased a radio for sixty-nine dollars and ninety-five cents cash. In the fourth floor front, the father of the family has not done a whole day's work in his life, and does not intend to. There are nine children, supported by the local parish. There is a tenth one on its way. . . .[47]

Her contempt is shared by Howard Roark and John Galt. Roark believes that the poor do not mind being packed together closely on public beaches because they are used to the smell of their flesh.[48] Galt, the "mind strike" leader of *Atlas Shrugged*, resents the fact that he subsidizes gin-swilling ne'er do-wells and other subhumans.[49]

Rand agrees with Banfield that the poor are not future-oriented. Rational people, on the other hand (such as Objectivists), see their interests in terms of a lifetime and select their goals accordingly. Short-range planning carries the possibility that one may just drift like a bum, spurred only by concerns of the moment.[50] She attributes this lack of planning partly to the poor's tendency to be manipulated by various schemers. These manipulators are found in Rand's novels, from the Communist party propagandizing for

worker-peasant unity in *We the Living* to left-lining Ellsworth
Toohey, the long-winded anti-individualist and cardboard villain
of *The Fountainhead*.[51] Perhaps the worst panderer to the poor and
their awful tastes is Gail Wynand, the editor of the New York *Ban-
ner* in *The Fountainhead*. In one edition, for example, he runs a
crusade against utility companies, a horoscope, excerpts from ser-
mons, leggy pictures of women, sensational, trashy stories about
lovers' quarrels ending in death, poems extolling the household
chores of women, and other similar trivial and exploitative features
and articles. These accounts, of course, fit mass taste; the poor, and
a great deal of the rest of the public are condemned to it by their ig-
norance and by their own short-term planning and orientation.[52]

How can the poor escape their plight? One narrow channel open
to them, of course, is to be very creative and extraordinary, like
Howard Roark or John Galt, or, for that matter, even Gail Wynand. Wynand had a Hell's Kitchen background and was a gang
leader in his teen years. His life changed after he read the inspiring
Social Darwinism of Herbert Spencer. (He was a gang leader who
had his toughs steal books so that he could *read* them. Well, plot
lines, characterizations and credibility are not Rand's strengths.)[53]

Civil disobedience, another possible avenue for the poor to make
their case, is also closed to them, even when carried out most
peacefully. This cannot be permitted, according to Rand, because it
is an interference with property and other rights.[54] All pathways to
worker and class solidarity are illegitimate in Rand's eyes because
they interfere with the rights of others; they are irrational; they are
anticreative and anti-individualistic; and, instead of being honest
and spontaneous, they are a Pavlovian response to the manipula-
tion and insincerity of rabble-rousers.[55] Rand would agree with
Buckley that it is all-important to keep the poor away from revolutionary leaders who will only tell them how bad off they are. Like
Buckley, she believes that arousing discontents is merely a process
of manufacturing grievances. The poor must be told that they are
faring badly because they cannot find objective grievances
themselves.

There are apparently no positive steps the poor can take in their
own behalf, and certainly there is no collective action that gains
Rand's approval. The only thing the poor can do is to hope that

their condition will be bettered. It will be, according to Rand, if they rely upon the creative rich. In fact, they are doomed if they fail to rely upon these benefactors. Francisco d'Anconia describes this situation in *Atlas Shrugged*:

> We are the soul, of which railroads, copper mines, steel mills and oil wells are the body . . . [they carry out] the sacred function of supporting human life, but only so long as they remain our body, only so long as they remain the expression, the reward and the property of achievement. Without us, they are corpses and their sole product is poison, not wealth or food, the poison of disintegration that turns men into hordes of scavengers.[56]

The poor, and for that matter, all people, are faced with many sets of dichotomies in the world of Objectivism: the minds and the mindless, the altruistic and the creative, the charitable and the virtuous, the morality of the marketplace and the amorality of collectivism, the free society of capitalism and the slave societies sought by liberals, socialists and Fascists and, above all, the productive and the parasitical.[57]

Overriding all of these conflicts are the truths, the rational and objective premises upon which Rand's unique form of conservatism asserts itself. The greatest of all virtues, we are told, is selfishness, and the most virtuous of all acts is making money.[58] The greatest moral issue of our time is the fight for the preservation of capitalism.[59] The greatest obstacle to the creative spirit of people is other people.[60] These same premises shape Rand's urban vision.

Rand's Urban Vision

Anyone who reads Rand's novels knows about her love of cities. Her characters are city-dwellers and city-lovers. Her themes involve urban life in more than a merely casual way. Her descriptions offer loving portraits of the city, especially of New York City. She regards New York as the greatest city on earth with a skyline that is the most magnificent sight on earth. Rand also thinks the City of New York is an industrial achievement, built by the imagination of great people; and like all great cities, it is a "frozen shape of human courage—the courage of those . . . who thought for the first time of every bolt, rivet and power generator that went to make it."[61] Dominique Francon, a character with whom Rand identifies, has a compulsive attachment to the city. In one passage in *The Fountainhead*, Dominique, living in her fashionable suburban house, gets a sudden and uncontrollable compulsion to be in the city. She has to feel it, smell it, sense it—immediately.[62] Rand is much like Dominique, rejecting her comfortable California home,when she was a film writer, for a cramped New York City apartment. Later, after trying to live in the country near New York, Rand and her husband returned to the City and vowed never to leave it again.[63]

The city, of course, is not for everyone. In the case of Rand's characters, it is the weak-kneed and faint-hearted who are uneasy in the urban atmosphere. Peter Keating, an uncreative and parasitic architect in *The Fountainhead* knows, when looking at the city, that he fears it and has always feared it. But while such oafs as Keating have no commitment to the city (or to much of anything else), Rand's heroic types adore it. Some of them even invest in businesses in the Inner City when they know they are bound to lose their money, simply because they have an urban commitment.[64]

Rand's adoration of New York does not prevent her from praising Petrograd (now Leningrad) in *We the Living*. She likes that city because it represents a strong and deliberate triumph over nature. Petrograd was not built in bits and pieces; it is a single entity of marble, stone, and mortar put together in a grand design. She also points out that, unlike the docile and unappealing city of Moscow, which has a feminine gender in the Russian language, Petrograd has a masculine ending signifying its virility.[65] (This is not the only time that Rand is sexist in her writing; she talks, for example, of Howard Roark owning Dominique Francon.[66]) In Rand's view Petrograd is not the triumph over nature New York is; for Rand, New York is the splendor of our time and of every other time.

It should hardly be surprising that an architect is the hero of one of her two most important novels. Architecture defines not only cities, but entire societies for her; and Howard Roark indulges in a joyous architecture uplifting the human spirit. Rand opposes and denigrates "negative" art, her description of " 'compassionate' studies of depravity," misery, disease, disaster, and all the negatives of human existence.[67] That not worth contemplating (and these things never are, she says) is not worth re-creating. Roark's art and entire perspective is defined within contexts of creative integrity and an ultimate, long-range optimism. He believes that his buildings must be honest just as people must be honest and that the integrity of both is only preserved by paying attention to the closest details of any artistic venture.[68] Roark will not compromise, then, with anyone who wants him to do something other than that which he wants to do. At the same time, he does not oppose making money, and manages to enjoy his career because he works, almost always, on private enterprise ventures. Roark's art is profitable. In fact, it would not be very useful art if it were unprofitable, for art must be valued by its creator and by others and it cannot be subsidized, according to Rand, or made an object of public or private charity. Financing art in this way, she believes, leads only to corruption.[69]

Architecture is a useful subject for a Rand novel because it touches upon aesthetics, commerce, and a host of value questions. To Rand, architecture is individualism writ large upon the face of the city in its public buildings and monuments, so that it brings this important issue into play. Architecture has, in addition, a strong bond with industry and technology. Rand's books tell us that train stations and steel mills are temples. New York City rests in a "ring of sacred fires, the ring of smokestacks, gas tanks, cranes and high tension lines."[70] The good and strong characters of her novels, such as John Galt, Howard Roark, and Dagny Taggart, love industry, the railroads, and the technology of urban centers of trade and commerce. Dagny Taggart, for example, always feels a sense of joy when she looks at machines. Machines are alive to her, purposeful, a "moral code cast in steel."[71] Trains possess two of the great attributes of life—motion and purpose, says Rand, and one of her greatest thrills in life was riding in the engineer's compartment on the New York Central's Twentieth Century Limited. Like Ayn Rand, the Dagny Taggarts, Hank Reardens and John Galts of *Atlas Shrugged* are reminiscent of the Warner and Swasey ads that used to appear frequently in magazines, urging the combination of

investment, low or no taxes, and new machinery as our economic
salvation. Everything is going to get bigger and better and more efficient if we will only believe in a linear development of
technological progress and growth.[72] This linear development, in
fact, has both a practical and an aesthetic dimension, for Rand not
only believes in a straight line of growth and progress, but also that
this straightness, which is not found in nature, is symbolic of the
achievement of creative individualism and of its conquest of
nature. Dagny Taggart illustrates the point:

> A circle, she thought, is the movement proper to physical nature
> . . . there's nothing but circular motion in the inanimate universe
> around us, but the straight line is the badge of man, the straight
> line of geometrical abstraction that makes roads, rails and
> bridges, the straight line that cuts the curving aimlessness of
> nature by a purposeful motion from a start to an end . . . man's
> life must be a straight line of motion from goal to further
> goal. . . . [73]

The lives of Rand's purposeful heroes and heroines are a ramrod-
straight line of progress.

Unfortunately, Rand's discussions of art and architecture, urbanism and nature, and industry and machinery seem to be lacking
in sense as much as they are lacking in artistic quality. The
various odes to steel mills, trains, and power stations are ludicrous;
they recall the parodies of the worst Soviet propaganda literature
of the "boy loves girl loves tractor" type—put forth with all the
seriousness Rand can muster. It is hard to deny the importance of
factories and high tension wires, but it is harder to be ecstatic about
them without appearing to possess a sense of misplaced or irrelevant priorities and values. Rand's love of the city and of the
New York skyline is understandable, at least, because she considers
them, as they are meant to be, aesthetic achievements. But her love
of steel mills and hatred of trees, her love of billboards and hatred
of the countryside, and her ecstasy as she contemplates industry
and railroads, seem eccentric and absurd.[74]

Rand's urban vision, then, is unique in that it specifically rejects nature and communing with nature. Nature is to be mastered but not loved. When Howard Roark looks at granite, he imagines it in buildings. When he looks at trees, he sees them cut and made into houses.[75] Hank Rearden believes that the earth will not end millions of years from now when the sun burns out because by that time people will be able to replace the sun.[76]

The earth is good, says Rand, because it is a limitless supplier. Still she adores industry so much that she hates the environmentalists. People should not curse industry for the smoke, fumes, or noise since this pulsating glow of life is far better than the void of economic decay and idleness. She urges people to embrace the smokestacks and whiff the fumes![77]

Environmentalism is anticapitalist, anti-urban and, most assuredly, anti-individualism, according to Rand. It upsets the romance of boy-loves-girl-loves-tractor, of billboards, of steelmill temples. Rand views the wedding of the city with industry, technology, and capitalism through a strange prism. Her novels tell us that this marriage is accomplished through the heroic and creative efforts of her leading characters and of people like them; but have such people ever existed? American history has no equivalent of Nat Taggart, who founded a railroad and operated it without any government assistance. Nat even throws a man who offers him a loan from the government down three flights of stairs, proving that assault and battery are preferable to the immorality of accepting such assistance.[78] Rand views Cornelius Vanderbilt, founder of the New York Cental Railroad, who might be considered some kind of real-life counterpart of Taggart, as one who engaged in a principled kind of corruption when he bribed state legislators and other officials in order to obtain franchises and other favors. "It is important to note," says Rand, "that the railroad owners did not start in business by corrupting the government. They had to turn to the practice of bribing legislators only in self-protection."[79] This kind of compromise, not to mention the historical revisionism, meets Rand's approval; she considers business cooperation with the Federal Trade Commission or the Anti-Trust Division of the Justice Department as the wrong kind of compromise.

Rand's urban vision is therefore based upon a romantic view of cities, industry, technology, and capitalism. It is further based upon a limited view of what constitutes creativity; and it leaves no place for group effort, social welfare legislation, or conventional politics. Her urban vision excludes the values of agrarian life and denigrates the beauty of nature because these contain few human achievements. Her view is also optimistic, believing in the correctness of Objectivist principles and in their guidance down an unwavering path of progress. Hers is a strange and paradoxical urban vision, enshrining the individual effort to the total exclusion of any kind of collective venture or cause and denying the complex interdependence and collective nature which characterize the life of all cities.

Rand's Urban Policies

The premises of Objectivism foreclose most urban policy choices for its adherents. Since Rand does not believe in any policy that involves social welfare or transfer payments, the government can do little in the urban arena. She indicates that only public safety functions are legitimate; therefore the role of government is extremely limited. Government involvement in any economic policymaking runs up against what Rand considers the maintenance of personal liberty, even though this noninterference may result in human suffering. The essence of Rand's conservatism can be found in the practical results of the policies (perhaps one should say nonpolicies) that flow from Objectivist principles. Her faith in Objectivism apparently overcomes any qualms she may have about suffering humanity. It will suffer much more, she thinks, with governmental involvement in the economy. Neither interested in hard data nor in society, she never seems curious, in any of her writings, about testing an Objectivist model or even in trying to infer possible social results from available hard data. Rand focuses on the indivudial. She likes Herbert Spencer and Social Darwinism and makes no bones about believing in the innate superiority of some of us and the inferiority of others.

Rand is an advocate of civil liberties in a limited sense. She knows that government policy, the economy, and just plain luck fall unequally upon various people but does not care. She strongly opposes measures like the draft, censorship, or the curtailing of sexual practices based upon consent. She does not oppose capital punishment, placing herself in the anomalous position of supporting the taking of life by the government, but not the taking of property.[80]

Nor does Rand's libertarianism extend to support for democracy. Democratic systems may incorporate guarantees of minority rights along with majority rule, but the adherence to voting, interest group politics, and an anti-ideological pluralism make such systems victimized by the spirit of compromise.[81] Rand is not one who trims many of her demands for the sake of compromise, except in the rather blatant case of bribery perpetrated by railroad officials illustrated above. As with Buckley, democracy is merely method. Any political system must run on more than this, and for Rand, this means it must recognize reality. Reality is, of course, Objectivism, that rational set of rules and conduct for society and for individuals based upon self-interest. Even though Rand pays lip service to the marketplace of ideas in her demands for liberty for everyone she does not really think that the marketplace will produce any set of rules or ideas that will surpass self-interest in importance or virtue.[82]

Writing fiction lets Rand argue her case in the best of all possible worlds. Straw villains like Ellsworth Toohey mouth witless remarks like ". . . we're all equal and interchangeable," making the task of the great Objectivist absurdly simple.[83] Howard Roark is served up with collectivist arguments so full of holes that his doctrines of selfishness and dog-eat-dog sound fairly reasonable. This in turn leads to policy pronouncements such as Roark's position on housing: there should be no public housing or housing subsidies, housing is only possible for the very rich and the very poor in our big cities because of such programs, and the middle-class taxpayer is supporting the "poor" parasites with his or her hard-earned money. In this particular case, there is enough truth, at least as far as public perception of the housing issue is concerned, to justify Roark's, hence Rand's, analysis. Roark is saying this in a novel published during World War II, but Rand supplies us with the same analysis to this day. The problems of the cities may change, and certainly housing problems and policy have undergone numerous and even drastic changes since that time, but Objectivism is steady, unswerving and timeless.

On race relations, the major issue affecting city politics and government in the past several decades, Rand holds a position that seems commendable when stated in abstract terms but which is racist in its practical results. She has excoriated conservatives many times for their racism, stating that denial of human rights on such an irrational basis destroys any conservative claims on other issues of rights, including property rights. At the same time, she claims that blacks and civil rights activists have promoted statism by demanding antiracist measures affecting employment, housing, and equality of opportunity. She dismisses "quotas" and affirmative action programs as immoral, racist, and futile. She believes that redress of the grievances of racial minorities cannot be legislated.[84]

Rand's antiracism often appears to be very weak and at best naive. Not only is she unconcerned about equality, but also she does not worry about equality of opportunity. Other values hold a higher place in her set of priorities. Perhaps this unconcern is best shown by her occasional ethnocentric lapses when her heroic characters speak of savage and uncivilized societies.[85] Rand speaks from a shockingly narrow cultural base that denies the values of Eastern, nonindustrial and nonurban societies.

Rand also seems unconcerned about sexual equality. She tells us that Howard Roark owns Dominique Francon.[86] Poor Dominique, a leading *Fountainhead* character, never even gets a part of the book named for her; all of these titles are reserved for males, including such bad guys as Ellsworth Toohey. In *Atlas Shrugged*, Dagny Taggart's clothes are described in one scene in which "the diamond band on the wrist of her naked arm gave her the most feminine of all aspects: the look of being chained."[87] Individualism can apparently go too far when sought by a female character in one of Ayn Rand's books and can only be expressed and lived to its ultimate by males. One might argue that Rand is representative only of the times in which she wrote these novels. With some writers, such an explanation might be plausible (though never excusable); but with Rand, who knows the rules of rationality and allegedly practices them as much as she advocates them, this is not permissable. Rand misses the vital point that equality of opportunity is a necessary *precondition* for the complete assertion of individuality of a woman, a member of a racial or ethnic minority, or a member of whatever group. Her toleration of inequality is, in addition, an acceptance of an irrational condition of life imposed by others against the individual well-being of those who are so oppressed. The self-interest of the oppressed, and surely self-interest must be a guideline to action as far as Rand is concerned, dictates the need for equality and for equality of treatment; and experience has amply demonstrated that obtaining these requires a measure of state intervention.

Rand's outlook on labor unions has some curious characteristics but is essentially reactionary. She does seem to understand the right to strike. One of her admirable characters, Austen Heller in *The Fountainhead*, believes in this right and puts his belief into practice.[88] There is a logical consistency for Rand in this position, since *Atlas Shrugged* is based upon the plot of a "mind strike" by industrial leaders. What is fair for one group in society ought to be fair for another. Labor unions should only function, however, on a voluntary basis, according to Rand.[89] This makes the jungle of labor relations even more complicated, as anyone familiar with the topic knows. Employers carry out warfare against unions under all conditions, whether membership is voluntary, contracted under "union shop" conditions, or coerced. Voluntary unionism is synonymous with weak unionism or no unionism. Unions therefore have little or no place in Rand's version of the City of the Right.

Rand not only believes that labor unions must be completely voluntary; she believes that all taxation systems must also be voluntary. The proper services of government, as she sees it, are the police, the armed forces and the law courts, and the need for these is both self-evident and based upon self-interest, the most important rational test. It is therefore reasonable that people will voluntarily pay for such services. She admits that this idea is premature at the moment, and that the voluntary financing of government is the last, rather than the first, step on the road to what she calls a free society.[90] The myriad of difficulties with this proposal do not need to be tackled at this point, she asserts, since nearly all of the other aspects of her utopian scheme would have to be in place as a precondition to its workability. This Poujadist idea demonstrates how close to anarchy Rand is willing to tread.

Education is not a legitimate function of government in Rand's eyes. Like Banfield, Buckley, Friedman, Kristol, and other conservatives, she has a particularly strong disdain for the

American public education system. She denies that there is such a thing as a "right" to an education.[91] She believes that education, like taxation and labor union membership, is a voluntary matter entered into freely by those who wish to organize it.[92]

Rand sets her civil libertarianism aside to point out that teachers and professors should be careful about what is taught. The public, and certainly no voluntary association, should hardly be required to finance views which are considered antagonistic to the interests of those who are paying the salaries.[93] Academic freedom is incompatible with Rand's view of what constitutes a "proper" education system. At the same time, ironically, she believes that too many professors are guilty of intellectual cowardice and that the few advocates of free enterprise capitalism remaining in our educational institutions face discrimination and prejudice.[94] All of these problems can be solved, however, if we "bring the field of education into the market-place" and apply Adam Smith competitive principles to its administration.[95] She likes voucher systems, private schools, and voluntarism, and she wants educators who will toe the line and teach what should be properly taught.

For the time being, Rand recognizes that we are trapped in the "mixed economy" of the welfare state, a system that she believes breeds corruption, including the corruption of compromise. This construct of the liberals and do-gooders will lead eventually, she says, to Fascism in America, not to a Socialist state or society. In this assessment, she can find a great deal of agreement from the Left in America, especially when she asserts that electing politicians to office in this system requires no program from them. It simply gives them a blank check with which to exercise power.[96]

The question to ask of Rand is whether her Objectivism represents any kind of worthwhile alternative for our society, particularly for the urban society she seems most to care about. She advocates freedom, but what kind of freedom? "*Freedom* in a political context . . . does *not* mean freedom from the landlord or freedom from the laws of nature. . . ." Instead, "it means freedom from the coercive power of the state—and nothing else."[97] Government-imposed coercion, however, seems only to mean economic coercion. Rand leaves the coercive mechanisms of the state intact, and feels no qualms about advocating their use for any cause she deems worthwhile, from capital punishment to the dismantling of labor unions. She leaves the coercive mechanisms of corporate power intact and sings hymns of praise to them. And she cares not a whit about air quality, consumers' rights, anti-discrimination laws, or the plight of the poor.

This is a sad and strange set of policies to derive from one whose urban vision is so romantic and powerful. In the end, Rand cares only about the physical structures in the cities. Paradoxically, she adores cities but cares little about the people living in them.

Notes

1. James Conaway, "Hollywood on the Potomac," *New York Times Book Review* (January 11, 1981), p. 11.

2. Wiliam F. O'Neill, *With Charity Toward None* (New York: Philosophical Library, 1971), p. 4.

3. Ibid., p. 4-6.

4. Ibid., pp. 16-17.

5. Jerome Tuccille, *It Usually Begins With Ayn Rand* (New York: Stein and Day, 1971), p. 19. In a letter to the author dated November 17, 1980, Tibor R. Machan, Rand scholar, author, and editor of *Reason*, states his "reasons for challenging the characterization of Rand as a conservative . . . these include Rand's atheism, her Aristotelian rationalism, her defense of natural rights [as against, e.g., Burke], her belief that human beings are not inherently evil [as against Russell Kirk], her anti-authoritariansim [as against Thomas Molnar] her egoism [as against virtually every conservative I know of], her capitalism [as against Irving Kristol's wishy-washy support of the same], and her very strong support of technology [as against the threat conservatives see in this type of materialism] . . . Also, I really trust Rand when she emphatically denies that she is a conservative. . . ."

6. Ayn Rand, *Capitalism—The Unknown Ideal* (New York: New American Library, 1967), p. 210; O'Neill, *With Charity Toward None*, p. 16.

7. O'Neill, *With Charity Toward None*, p. 16.

8. Ayn Rand, *The Virtue of Selfishness* (New York: New American Library, 1964), p. 122.

9. Ibid., pp. 180-81.

10. Tuccille, *It Usually Begins With Ayn Rand,* p. 167.

11. Rand, *Capitalism-The Unknown Ideal*, p. 215.

12. O'Neill, *With Charity Toward None*, pp. 33-34.

13. Ayn Rand, *We The Living* (New York: New American Library, 1959 edition), p. vii.

14. See Rand's introduction in *We The Living*; also, Nathaniel Branden, *Who is Ayn Rand?* (New York: Random House, 1962), p. 168.

15. Nathaniel Branden, *Who Is Ayn Rand?*, p. 169; Ayn Rand, *We The Living*, p. 132.

16. Branden, *Who Is Ayn Rand?*, p. 172.

17. Branden, *Who is Ayn Rand?*. p. 173. It is interesting to reflect upon this association, since there is a great deal that Rand and the late DeMille can be said to share in any number of ways: a romanticism in their art, a sense of grandeur and spectacle, the creation of events and characters that are larger than life, a tendency to substitute bigness for substance or quality, a decided mediocrity, and a virulent antilabor union attitude found in Rand's books and in the shaping of some aspects of DeMille's career.

18. Ibid., p. 211.

19. Ibid., p. 150; Ayn Rand, *Atlas Shrugged* (New York: Random House, 1957), p. 1085.

20. Rand, *We The Living*, p. 388.

21. Rand, *Atlas Shrugged*, p. 680.

22. Rand, *The Fountainhead* (New York: Bobbs-Merrill, 1943), p. 301.

23. Rand, *For the New Intellectual* (New York: New American Library, 1961), p. 58.

24. Rand, *Atlas Shrugged*, p. 579.

25. O'Neill, *With Charity Toward None,* p. 18.

26. Rand, *The Virtue of Selfishness*, p. 57.

27. Ibid., p. 123.

28. Ibid., pp. 135-38.

29. Rand, *The Fountainhead*, p. 672.

30. Quoted in O'Neill, *With Charity Toward None,* p. 209.

31. Rand, *Virtue of Selfishness*, pp. 106-8, 127-29.

32. Rand, *Capitalism—The Unknown Ideal,* pp. 206-9.

33. Rand, *Atlas Shrugged*, p. 870.

34. Ibid., p. 220.

35. Rand, *The Fountainhead*, p. 190.

36. O'Neill, *With Charity Toward None,* p. 197.

37. Rand, *Atlas Shrugged,* p. 224.

38. Quoted in O'Neill, *With Charity Toward None,* p. 48.

39. Rand, *Virtue of Selfishness*, p. 119.

40. Rand, *The Fountainhead*, p. 302, 439 and 479 are good examples.

41. Rand, *The Fountainhead*, pp. 311-312, 326.

42. Rand, *Virtue of Selfishness*, p. 118.

43. This is not a matter of taking sides between various kinds of exploiters; it is merely a matter of pointing out the one of Rand's illogical assumptions.

44. Rand, *Virtue of Selfishness*, pp. 104, 151-54, 158-60.

45. In *The Fountainhead*, p. 158, hero Roark states that the public gets "what it wants" because it takes what is given to it without thinking about it. The world is full of "vague, fat, blind inertia."

46. Rand, *The Fountainhead*, p. 136.

47. Ibid., p. 133.

48. Ibid., p. 499.

49. Rand, *Atlas Shrugged*, p. 713.

50. Rand, *Virtue of Selfishness*, p. 60.

51. To Toohey, the workers are the most important of all social elements; *The Fountainhead*, p. 467. The statements Rand puts into the mouths of her villains are as interesting as those she ascribes to her heroes. A whole set of Toohey tastes and opinions are set out in *The Fountainhead*, p. 297.

52. Rand, *The Fountainhead*, p. 68.

53. Ibid., pp. 394, 398.

54. O'Neill, *With Charity Toward None,* p.218.

55. Rand, *Virtue of Selfishness,* pp. 127-38.

56. Rand, *Atlas Shrugged*, p. 580.

57. Rand, *The Fountainhead*, p. 673; *Capitalism—The Unknown Ideal,* p. 41.

58. Rand, *The Virtue of Selfishness*; *Atlas Shrugged*, p. 96.

59. Rand, *For the New Intellectual*, p. 63.

60. Nathaniel Branden, *Who Is Ayn Rand?*, p. 197.

61. Rand, *Atlas Shrugged*, p. 481; also, see *Atlas Shrugged*, pp. 194, 906; *The Fountainhead*, p. 439, and the urban descriptions in *The Fountainhead*, pp. 84, 92, 192, and 302.

62. Rand, *The Fountainhead*, p. 235. Ayn Rand states that "Dominique is myself in a bad mood," according to Branden, *Who Is Ayn Rand?*, p. 195.

63. Branden, *Who Is Ayn Rand?*, p. 226.

64. Rand, *The Fountainhead*, pp. 77, 159, 168-69.

65. Rand, *We The Living*, p. 229; also see pp. 23-24, 149, 226-27.

65. Rand, *We the Living*, p. 229; also see pp. 23,-24, 149, 226-27.

66. Branden, *Who Is Ayn Rand?*, p. 195.

67. Ayn Rand, *The Romantic Manifesto: A Philosophy of Literature* (New York and Cleveland: World, 1970), p. 167.

68. Rand, *The Fountainhead*, p. 189.

69. Rand, *Virtue of Selfishness*, p. 133.

70. Rand, *Atlas Shrugged*, p. 260.

71. Branden, *Who Is Ayn Rand?*, p. 132.

72. See, for example, Ellis Wyatt on oil shale in Rand, *Atlas Shrugged*, p. 237.

73. Ibid., pp. 569-70.

74. On the love of billboards, see ibid., pp. 266-67.

75. Rand, *The Fountainhead*, p. 8.

76. Rand, *Atlas Shrugged*, p. 165.

77. Ibid., p. 1005; Tuccille, *It Usually Begins with Ayn Rand*, p. 175-76.

78. Rand, *Atlas Shrugged*, p. 63.

79. O'Neill, *With Charity Toward None*, pp. 183-84.

80. Ibid., p. 207.

81. Rand, *Capitalism—The Unknown Ideal*, pp. 206-12.

82. O'Neill, *With Charity Toward None*, pp. 179-80, 183-84.

83. Rand, *The Fountainhead*, p. 562.

84. Rand, *Virtue of Selfishness*, pp. 172-85.

85. Rand, *For the New Intellectual*, p. 58; *Atlas Shrugged*, pp. 883, 965, 966, 976; *Virtue of Selfishness*, p. 142.

86. Branden, *Who is Ayn Rand?*, p. 195.

87. Rand, *Atlas Shrugged*, p. 133.

88. Rand, *The Fountainhead*, p. 100.

89. Rand, *Virtue of Selfishness*, p. 137.

90. Ibid., pp. 157-60.

91. Ibid., p. 129.

92. O'Neill, *With Charity Toward None*, pp. 220-21.

93. Rand, *Virtue of Selfishness*, p. 132.

94. Rand, *Atlas Shrugged*, p. 668.

95. O'Neill, *With Charity Toward None*, p. 220.

96. Rand, *Capitalism—The Unknown Ideal*, pp. 205, 212, 214.

97. O'Neill, *With Charity Toward None*, pp. 46-47.

7

THE CITY OF THE RIGHT

A broad spectrum of opinion, conservative and otherwise, seems to agree that the experience of the past two decades demonstrates the failure of liberal programs and policies in our cities. But the advent of the City of the Right can hardly be a cheering prospect. Liberalism has not worked, but conservatism appears to have virtually no prospect of success, either.

This does not mean that the ideas discussesd in the five previous chapters should be totally rejected. Some proposals, especially those which come from the fertile mind of Milton Friedman, are laudable or at least interesting possibilities. Elimination of tax loopholes is an honorable goal. Voucher systems could be applied to a variety of programs, and some interesting experiments of this kind are now being carried out.[1] Many experts would demur, however, on Friedman's voucher plan for the schools. The negative income tax also presents new opportunities for dealing with the problem of poverty, but replacing welfare programs with such a tax should be carefully examined to ensure that the poor would not be penalized by a cut in support. Both Friedman and Rand take strong positions on the civil liberties side of the censorship issue; and there are undoubtedly a few other matters in which the proposals of these five thinkers could prove helpful or progressive in terms of the cities and their needs.

None of the foregoing ideas, however, are the exclusive domain of conservatives. Most of them, or variations, have a measure of support from liberals or centrists or others. Perhaps the most attractive feature of modern American conservatism and of the views of these five writers is an attachment to "small government"—a belief in decentralized decision-making structures coupled with a strong antibureacratic bias. Democracy requires a closeness of government to the people. But this view gained wide currency on the Left during the 1960s, and has always been a tradition of some brands of socialism.[2] It is therefore necessary to probe a little deeper in order to ascertain the distinctive characteristics of the City of the Right.

Some general observations are in order. The five writers, first of all, have many beliefs and values that they hold in common. All five are laissez-faire Adam Smith disciples in their economic views. All five are probusiness and have a special liking for the giant, monopolistic firms that Adam Smith would have detested. They reject greater equality of incomes and, generally speaking, equality of opportunity as well. It is fair to call them ethnocentric to an absurd degree and, because of this, they line up behind racist policies and/or racist policy results. The writings of two of the five, Banfield and Buckley, can be characterized as racist.

These thinkers are intellectuals given to other-worldly abstractions that are often not the least bit pragmatic; and this is a grave failing for anyone who seeks to prescribe urban policies. All of these commentators on the city also live in cities, but—except for Rand—are not *of* the city; they have no special love for the city, only a utilitarian attitude towards it. Rand is different, of course, with her romantic attachment to tall buildings, smokestacks, and wide bridges. Hers is a kind of "neutron bomb" attitude, cherishing things while worrying very little about people.

The City of the Right quintet adheres to a belief in the line that supposedly separates "public" and "private." Government and "private" business firms are antagonists, not comrades or partners. There is an implicit, and occasionally explicit, rejection of C. Wright Mills's claim of the existence of a military-industrial complex or "power elite" system. Mills holds that the line between the federal bureaucracy and a so-called private bureaucracy like

General Motors or Lockheed is misleading, and that we actually have a corporate state. Such a view undermines the attachment these five have for big firms, however, and so there is a rejection of the corporate-state view as a fantasy of the present; it is seen more as a threat of the future. Friedman and Kristol seem most aware of the government-industry connection; at least they write more about it. And even these two diverge: Friedman decries such connections because they interfere with the Smithian model, while Kristol has a resigned attitude towards the inevitability of it.

In any event the five, like many other conservatives, have their own myths about a power elite. They use various terms to describe it, but Irving Kristol's characterization, the "new class," is specifically endorsed by Buckley and Friedman, and it seems clear that Banfield and Rand would be comfortable with it as well. The "new class," though it is often used in an imprecise way, is an antibusiness, antiprofit consortium of media people, bureaucrats, academics, and intellectuals. And the existence of this "new class" explains, for all of the five, a great deal about what is wrong with America. Ellsworth Toohey, the cardboard villain of Ayn Rand's *The Fountainhead*, perhaps represents the kind of person usually borne in mind when this "new class" term is used.

But what will the City of the Right be like? Assuming that most or all of the measures proposed by its proponents have been adopted, it is not difficult to summon up images. An urban resident, on a typical day, leaves home to go to work. She or he lives in a segregated neighborhod, since this is a typical residential pattern and boundaries of the metropolitan area's various cities and suburbs would be deliberately left intact. Segregation would have an additional impetus, however, from the limited role played by government in housing and urban development and from the proliferation of private schools at the expense of public education. This urban citizen may face a long wait for the bus. Public transportation would be operating on a shoestring, if at all, since it does not "pay for itself" and since private entrepreneurs long ago demonstrated their unwillingness to be involved with its service. Plenty of police would be in evidence, and garbage would frequently be piled up on the streets. Air pollution would be obvious, and various irritating (and often toxic) substances would be mixed with particulates in the atmosphere because industry would not be regulated closely. Cars, archaic as they are as a means of urban transport, would abound. The only alleviation of this air pollution would be the movement of factories to the Sun Belt or foreign locations, a process encouraged by the City of the Right.

At work, the urban resident would notice, quite frequently, the substandard condition of public services. All residents of the metropolis rely upon these services during working hours, even if they are suburbanites blessed with better services at home. Working conditions might not be so pleasant, either, since all or most occupational safety protections would have been abolished. Worker safety is a matter for the market to define. Wages might be quite low because the pressures of unions on wage rates would have been reduced or abolished. In addition, repeal of the minimum wage, advocated by all of the City of the Right thinkers, would have wage-depressing effects upon the entire job market, for adults and teenagers alike. Unemployment among youths would probably be greater, because some of the teen-age jobs would be taken by adults.[3]

After stopping at a shop to pick up one or two untrustworthy consumer products (because most safety and quality regulations would have been repealed) the weary urbanite would again face the difficult problem of transportation home. Infrequent bus or subway service or a breakdown of equipment would often be the reasonable expectation. Home life would be plagued with worries wrought by low wages, the lack of consumer and worker protections, and the degeneration of public services.

Quality of education would hardly be assured by the conservative remedies of segregation and voucher systems. The crime rate could be expected to soar, although draconian police state measures would surely be put into effect. If the City of the Right happened to be Banfield's Unheavenly City, it would not be wise to trust television news coverage of crime or current events because this would be subject to a rigid censorship.

Any sense of community or even the rudimentary obligations of citizenship would be hard put to survive under these circumstances. Hierarchy and class rule would be more evident than ever. Income disparities, already widening, would widen further, although taxes might be lower. The tax system, however it might be administered, would operate on a flat rate or regressive basis; that is, without reference to the criterion of ability to pay.

What has been omitted from the City of the Right programs of our five principals is just as important as what is emphasized. It is not possible to fault them for not writing about subjects we may care to see covered, but it is fair to list some of the urban issues and concerns commonly accepted as pressing considerations today and to array these against the contributions of the five. This provides a clearer view of their emphases.

The problems of delivery of urban services and programs are never mentioned; these are significant issues that receive a great deal of attention from urban specialists.[4] The related issue of the need for public works is also never broached, even though the condition of America's streets, sanitation facilities, water systems, bridges, port facilities, and correctional facilities are all in alarming states of deterioration. A new study by the Council of State Planning Agencies shows that the process of "re-industrialization," which is so loudly blared through the trumpets of conservative politicians, is dependent upon the renewal of this public works base.[5] This point was made two decades ago in John Kenneth Galbraith's *The Affluent Society*;[6] it was not heeded then, and matters have grown much worse since that time.

Environmental issues, save for a few nasty asides about environmentalists and Friedman's pollution tax, are given very little attention. Kristol borrows the useless argument of "Pogo-ism" and applies it to the city environment.

The urgent question of metropolitan boundaries and the problems these artificial barriers cause in terms of taxation, education, services delivery, and equality of services gets scant attention. Kristol notes the problem. Buckley and Banfield, however, actually applaud the flight to the suburbs which has occurred since World War II. They therefore place themselves in the ridiculous position of applauding *de facto* segregation, and they have no apparent sympathy for policies, such as busing, designed to deal with it. The danger of continuing this state of affairs is ignored. The right of social mobility, which is closely linked with physical mobility, is likewise ignored, though this is not merely a fault of conservatives.

This lack of mobility helps to account for suburbanization, for the development of enclaves hospitable to only certain social and economic categories of people, and for the denigration of the rights of the elderly, the handicapped, and minorities, who are assigned to certain types of ghettoes by our social and political systems.

Another right of mobility issue, immigration, which has had a great impact on many cities in recent years, is also ignored, although Buckley and Friedman make feeble stabs at it. Buckley decries immigration on neo-Nativist grounds; Friedman takes a much more tolerant view and notes that immigration, legal or not, is a response to job market conditions.

It is hardly surprising that the question of how we may divide up the wealth in a zero-sum society—a society tied to an economy which no longer grows—is never raised. The assumption of economic growth on a sustained basis into the indefinite future makes division of wealth easier because the pie keeps growing. But there are strong signs that this may not occur, and economists such as Lester Thurow have at least done some thinking about this.[7] Conservatives, generally speaking, have not.

The issue of "regional shift" is noted, but only long enough to applaud this development. The loss of jobs, industry, and population to the South and Southwest from the Northeast and Midwest is considered positively. The socially responsible, heavily unionized states deserve to take it on the chin. Friedman makes it clear that regional shift is a long-standing policy *goal* of some conservatives. This had begun to dawn upon residents of the Northeast and Midwest. One unemployed worker recently stated, for example, that "all these people want to do is drive workers to the Sun Belt where they'll take any job at any wage no matter what."[8]

Finally, it should be stressed that while most of these concerns and issues are overlooked and sometimes missing altogether on the Right, there is also a complete lack of understanding of the importance of the preeminent urban issue, race relations. Race relations are discussed at considerable length by all five subjects; but the talk is usually in terms of advice to blacks, of how much better off blacks are today than they used to be, of how discrimination is abated by the dynamics of the free market, or of how to repress black anger and resentment caused by unfair treatment. Only Rand seems to demonstrate any awareness of the sorry record of conservatives on the issue of minority rights.

The City of the Right's advocates provide fairly uniform economic prescriptions for the city. There is less divergence in this policy area than in any other; perhaps it can be assumed that they are guided by an "invisible hand." As is already pointed out, conservatives would do away with the minimum wage. If this is not possible, they would reduce it, especially for teenagers. They would also end most or all consumer protections devised by agencies such as the Federal Trade Commission and by the workplace rules of the Occupational Safety and Health Administration. Laissez-faire is the guide. Management of urban development and housing policies would be left to the economy's private sectors; the arguments for this can be illustrated with truly horrible examples of urban renewal, urban development action grants, and similar policies. But business has always been free to come into the city and lend its skills and resources to the task of rebuilding. And the best available recent tests of a complete, or nearly complete, laissez-faire model of development can be found in the states of Arizona and New Mexico, where chaos, land fraud, and even gangsterism have reigned unchecked, to the detriment of social and environmental needs.[9] Transportation is also crudely fitted to a laissez-faire model, with the car as the centerpiece. This is a hopeless position in the long run, since public transportation is much more economical when environmental, traffic control, enforcement, and energy considerations are weighed. In addition, Buckley, Friedman and other conservatives would skew the economy with a selective and class-based law enforcement that would use anti-trust statutes to break up unions but would limit the use of such laws against corporations.

Ceaseless arguments proceed from the economic prescriptions posited here. And it seems that no one with strong views about economic policies, including economists, is ever satisfied that his or her prescriptions have been tried or tested adequately. It is finally a question of empirical proofs and the standards developed to measure such proofs. One could say that not one of these prescriptions has been tested or proved; we are justified, all the same, in being dubious about them. On the one hand, the economic models developed or influenced by conservatives—and there is an abundance of them, in pre-1930 America, in Margaret Thatcher's Britain, in post-Allende Chile, and in various American states in which conservative policies hold sway—are not encouraging, and they are especially not encouraging for cities.[10] On the other hand, it should be admitted that, uneasy as we all must be about the welfare state, it appears that it has at least worked better than our five experts would care to acknowledge. Although there are approaches other than the values, dimensions, and parameters of the current welfare state system that we can apply to our urban society if we muster up the imagination and courage to try them, the welfare state has managed to alleviate and, on occasion, to eradicate human suffering. The removal of its minimal floors and guarantees, flimsy though these are, could bring on widespread misery.

The greatest indictment of the City of the Right, however, is that it is a place in which many of the liberties most of us take for granted are threatened or abolished. All through this study, this point has been noted whenever the writings of Banfield, Buckley, Friedman, Kristol, and Rand have made themselves painfully plain.

Anti-libertarianism takes many forms. It shows up most obviously in the discussions of crime. Crime is a real problem in our cities, no mistake about it. But are the kinds of crackdowns and suspensions of liberties, especially as advanced by Banfield and Buckley, the ways to deal with the situation?

One prudent observer has suggested that the belligerent writing on foreign policy produced by some of these five is a key to understanding their anti-libertarianism. Their readiness to reach for the quick, firm military response to our perceived enemies abroad is obvious if you read their articles or columns over a period of time. Buckley's *National Review* columns and Kristol's *Wall Street Journal* columns supply pointed examples. Their tendency to reach for a quick, firm, and again, military response to the "enemies" of society in our cities is the same behavior pattern reproduced in a different environment. But there is a logic at work here as well, for those who are used to practicing brinksmanship in foreign policy are not likely to shy away from its use in the urban arena.[11]

The only commendable feature of this anti-libertarianism is its frankness. Banfield says he favors controls on the media. Friedman and Kristol are outspoken in their support of represive measures for urban college campuses. Banfield and Buckley clearly set out their belief that, under a number of circumstances, forced deportations of people from the city are proper and desirable; and these people, it should be added, are people who would not have committed a crime in most cases.

The attack on the welfare state is intimately bound up with this anti-libertariansim. The welfare state, after all, does provide a measure of freedom of opportunity and a measure of economic freedom for those who benefit from welfare, Head Start, food stamps, aid to the blind, or other social services. But it is bound up in another way. A dynamic is set in motion by attacks on the welfare state and even by cuts in various welfare programs, for these actions produce a reaction. Many observers of urban America have known, and have pointed out, that " . . . the long-term curtailment of the welfare state is radically unlikely without political repression."[12] Removal of income floors, medical care, housing programs, day-care centers, and poverty programs from an urban community is likely to bring about strong protest, and if people become desperate, they will do desperate things. And, as pointed out on several occasions, these conservatives never believe that the poor or the desperate act on their own. Someone, they insultingly insist, has to tell them how bad off they are and has to "stir them up" with rabblerousing activities. Confronted with even fairly mild protest, conservatives will call for repression. Their writings demonstrate this willingness beyond any doubt. What else can they do? Reinstate the programs they propose to cut or abolish? Not likely. They would sooner spend greater amounts on the personnel and tools needed to carry out repression. The dynamic of large-scale urban repression begins, then, with this antiwelfare-state recipe of induced chaos and protest.

Why does this dynamic exist? Are conservatives incapable of understanding the late twentieth-century American city and the needs and aspirations of its people? Comb through the outpourings of our five or almost any other important conservative writers and thinkers and, sad to say, this is indeed the case. Conservatism and urban values do not fit together very well; indeed, they seem to be on a collision course. Why?

A search for the answer leads to any number of plausible explanations: The agrarian values of conservative thought in America, the tendency of important thinkers, conservative and otherwise, to denigrate the city, the misleading fantasies about a "new class," the square peg of Adam Smith economics and the insistence upon implanting it into the decidedly un-square city, the impatience and petulance of the privileged, the inability to adjust to social and cultural change, the racism.

The two most important considerations accounting for the failure of conservatives to understand the city and its needs, however, are found in the very bone and marrow of conservatism itself: the quest for authority, sometimes just for its own sake, and the insistence upon inequality, not only in the so-called natural state of affairs, but in the treatment of people by society, by the state, and by the law.

Inequality figures strongly in the urban visions and policy prescriptions of Banfield, Buckley, Friedman, Kristol, and Rand. It can invariably be shown to be part and parcel of the thought of any other important conservative political or intellectual figure. Inequality is one of the defining characteristics of conservatism. It could be objected that criticism of conservatives on this score is akin to criticism of socialists for demanding equality or of Quakers for being pacifists. But the point is that inequality is a value which does not coexist easily with urban values. It is alien.

The quest for authority is a concern extending beyond conservatism, although the emphasis upon the need for authority seems to be most pronounced in conservative writings. In recent years, people of every political persuasion have been impressed by the serious breakdown of authority occurring in American urban life. None of the five thinkers selected for this study, unfortunately, have grappled with this as well as another conservative, Robert Nisbet, has:

It would be comforting if the revolt were simply the result of Vietnam and Watergate. But it cannot be so seen. In the first place the roots of revolt are deeper and older in this country. In the second place, precisely the same kind of revolt is to be seen in other Western countries, those which have known neither Vietnam nor Watergate. . . . Clearly, we are at the beginning of a new Reformation . . . one that has the political state rather than the church as the central object of its force; a force that ranges from the slow drips of apathy to the more hurricane-like intensities of violence and terror. The first great Reformation, that of the sixteenth century, was also a period of twilight of authority in the West.[13]

This authority can be reestablished, says Nisbet, through a sense of community, the pluralism which incorporates a clear division of public and private life, a sense of social obligation, kinship ties, voluntary associations, and, most interesting, a revival of localism: "Even in a city like New York, there is far more neighborhood community than we commonly give it credit for in the country at large."[14] And perhaps this is so; perhaps authority can be reestablished and perhaps it is even desirable that authority should be reestablished. It must be remembered, however, that rebelliousness against authority should not be invariably condemned. A great many of the protests of the 1960s and 1970s in urban America should be applauded, not condemned. A number of urban observers even believe that social and political gains achieved by these protests could never have been possible through conventional political means. And society as a whole, not just the groups and people directly involved, may have benefited from these developments.

Nisbet goes on to add two more requisites for the reestablishment of authority: laissez-faire economics and hierarchy.[15] He is, after all, a conservative; he does not recognize that these are among the causes of social alienation and civic unrest, which makes them strange cures. One of these, laissez-faire, is, as we have seen, a pipe dream, although this does not prevent it from causing great harm. The other, hierarchy, has its uses for those who wish to prevent social change or to redistribute wealth at the expense of the poor.

In many ways, however, hierarchy seems to be increasingly out of fashion because of the growth, albeit in fits and starts, of a late twentieth-century sensibility to the manifest fairness of social, political, and legal equality. Hierarchy, never easy to justify, may have hard times ahead.

The need for authority, though not as well stated as by Nisbet, is strongly agreed upon by Banfield, Buckley, Friedman, Kristol, and Rand. They feel this vacuum so badly, in fact, that they are willing to call for extreme measures to fill it. And in doing so, they largely vitiate their effectiveness as commentators on our urban condition and as analysts of our urban problems. Their policy proposals should not be given very much weight or credence. Their conservatism cannot be a basis for policy because it rests primarily upon a belief in an inequality which is pernicious if not impractical and upon a demand for authority which is tied to the forlorn hopes of laissez-faire anachronisms and an idea of hierarchy which achieves no justification.

Cities have been with us throughout the history of civilization, but they have never been so complex as they are today. They are intricate communications networks. They are interdependent economic entities and, perhaps above all, they are sensitive political and social communities. If our cities are ever to "work," they will require the forging of a cooperative spirit which mirrors the interdependent needs of their people. This requires a collective will. Cooperation, interdependence, and collective are terms which, unfortunately, are anathema to conservatives. As a result, they have fashioned a City of the Right that meets none of these needs and which can only be called uncaring, brutal, divisive, and inhumane. A City of the Right can only be a city of the wronged.

Notes

1. Neal Peirce, "Minnesota's Right to 'Exit' Programs," Fort Wayne *Journal-Gazette*, December 7, 1980.

2. See, for example, Gerald L. Houseman, *G. D. H. Cole* (Boston: G. K. Hall, 1979).

3. These are the conclusions of a study by Alan Fisher, an economics professor at California State University at Fullerton, in 1975; for a brief explanation, see *Wall Street Journal*, February 8, 1981.

4. See, for example, Robert L. Lineberry, *Equality and Urban Policy: The Distribution of Municipal Public Services* (Beverly Hills, Calif.: Sage, 1977).

5. Pat Choate and Susan Walter, *America in Ruins: Beyond the Public Works Pork Barrel* (Washington: Council of State Planning Agencies, 1981).

6. John Kenneth Galbraith, *The Affluent Society* (Boston: Houghton Mifflin, 1958).

7. Lester Thurow, *The Zero-Sum Society: Distribution and the Possibilities for Economic Change* (New York: Basic Books, 1980).

8. *UAW (United Automobile Workers) Washington Report* 21 (March 13, 1981): 4.

9. Patricia A. Simko et al., *Promised Lands: Subdivisions and the Law*, vol. 3 (New York: Inform, 1978), pp. 139-214.

10. "Thatcher's Economic Woes—A Lesson for the U.S.?" *U.S. News and World Report*, March 2, 1981: 29-30.

11. These observations were made by a colleague who provided some ideas during the early stages of research on this work.

12. Michael Walzer, "Life with Father," *New York Review of Books* 28 (April 2, 1981): 4.

13. Robert Nisbet, *Twilight of Authority* (New York: Oxford University Press, 1975), pp. 5-6.

14. Ibid., p. 267.

15. Ibid., chapter 5. Also, see Richard Flathman, *The Practice of Political Authority: Authority and the Authoritative* (Chicago: University of Chicago Press, 1980).

BIBLIOGRAPHY

Banfield, Edward C. *The Unheavenly City*. Boston: Little, Brown, 1970.
_____. *The Unheavenly City Revisited*. Boston: Little, Brown, 1974.
Buckley, William F. Jr. *Execution Eve—and Other Contemporary Ballads*. New York: G. P. Putnam's Sons, 1975.
_____. *The Governor Listeth: A Book of Inspired Political Revelations*. New York: G. P. Putnam's Sons, 1970.
_____. *Inveighing We Will Go*. New York: G. P. Putnam's Sons, 1972.
_____. *The Jeweler's Eye*. New York: G. P. Putnam's Sons, 1968.
_____. *The Unmaking of a Mayor*. New York: Viking Press, 1966.
Coser, Lewis A., and Howe, Irving, eds. *The New Conservatives: A Critique from the Left*. New York: New American Library, 1973.
Franke, David, comp. *Quotations from Chairman Bill*. New Rochelle, N.Y.: Arlington House, 1970.
Friedman, Milton. *An Economist's Protest: Columns in Political Economy*. New York: Thomas Horton, 1972.
_____. *There's No Such Thing as a Free Lunch*. LaSalle, Ill.: Open Court, 1975.
Friedman, Milton, with Rose Friedman. *Capialism and Freedom*. Chicago: University of Chicago Press, 1962.
Friedman, Milton, and Friedman, Rose. *Free to Choose: A Personal Statement*. New York: Harcourt Brace Jovanovich, 1980.

Kristol, Irving. *On the Democratic Idea in America.* New York: Harper and Row, 1972.

_____. *Two Cheers for Capitalism.* New York: Basic Books, 1978.

Markmann, Charles L. *The Buckleys: A Family Examined.* New York: William Morrow, 1973.

O'Neill, William F. *With Charity Toward None.* New York: Philosophical Library, 1971.

Rand, Ayn. *Atlas Shrugged.* New York: Random House, 1957.

_____. *Capitalism: The Unknown Ideal.* New York: New American Library, 1967.

_____. *For the New Intellectual.* New York: New American Library, 1961.

_____. *The Fountainhead.* New York: Bobbs-Merrill, 1943.

_____. *The Virtue of Selfishness.* New York: New American Library, 1964.

_____. *We the Living.* New York: New American Library, 1959.

Steinfels, Peter. *The Neoconservatives.* New York: Simon and Schuster, 1979.

INDEX

204

About the Author

GERALD L. HOUSEMAN is Associate Professor of Political Science and Public and Environmental Affairs at Indiana University at Fort Wayne. His earlier writings include *G. D. H. Cole* and *The Right of Mobility*. He is the co-author, with H. Mark Roelofs, of *The American Political System: Ideology and Myth*.